Lifting the Curtain on Design

LIFTING
THE CURTAIN ON DESIGN

WORDS AND PHOTOGRAPHS BY

VICENTE
WOLF

WRITTEN WITH
Christine Pittel

The Monacelli Press

I dedicate this book to good and loyal friends:

Preston Bailey has been there in good times
and in bad. His joie de vivre, generosity
of spirit, and enormous talent have made him
a valuable and precious friend.

Richard and Jane Novick are not only great
clients but great friends. They have been
by my side since I first started my business.

———————

Copyright © 2010 by The Monacelli Press,
a division of Random House, Inc.
Text and photographs copyright © 2010 by
Vicente Wolf

Published in the United States by The Monacelli Press,
a division of Random House, Inc., New York

The Monacelli Press and the M design are registered
trademarks of Random House, Inc.

Library of Congress Cataloging-in-Publication Data
Wolf, Vicente.
Lifting the curtain on design / words and photographs
by Vicente Wolf ; written with Christine Pittel. — 1st ed.
p.   cm.
ISBN 978-1-58093-267-7
1. Interior decoration—Themes, motives. 2. Wolf,
Vicente—Travel. I. Pittel, Christine. II. Title.
NK2113.W573   2010
747—dc22   2010017731

Printed in China

www.monacellipress.com

10 9 8 7 6 5 4 3 2 1
First edition

Designed by Beverly Joel, pulp, ink.

INTRODUCTION

THERE WAS A PERIOD IN MY LIFE WHEN I DID NOT have a clue about who or what I wanted to be. I was completely disconnected from whatever talents I might have had. I was fortunate enough to meet Bob Patino, an interior designer who became a mentor to me. Very quickly, I found a direction and a career.

I immersed myself in work, and the years flew by. I was continually looking for the next job, the next challenge. The one constant in my schedule was an annual trip. Every December I visited some exotic destination. This was adventure travel, and it usually did not involve luxury hotels or pampering. The point was to get closer to another culture.

One year I was in the Himalayas, hiking through a rhododendron forest along the border between Sikkim and Nepal. The views were incredible, but the mountain path was more suited to goats than to people. It was a perpetual zigzag—climbing up, flattening out, then climbing up again. I was looking at the steep incline coming up and thinking about how I hate going uphill. When was it going to be lunchtime? How much farther did we have to go before it would be over? Why was I here?

All of a sudden a light bulb went off in my head. Wait a minute. I'm walking on the flat part now, and it's actually kind of pleasant. The clouds just parted, the sun came out, and I can feel the warmth on my skin. Why don't I enjoy it, instead of worrying about what's up ahead?

The future will always be just out of reach. You'll get there eventually, and it may not be as bad as you think. But in the meantime, don't miss the here and now. Live in the moment. That's what's important. What am I doing today? How can I use my energies?

I don't pretend to have absorbed this message completely, but I'm trying. There is always a before and an after; but the point is to be present and aware for all the moments in between.

SIMPLIFY

NAMIBIA

I had heard that Namibia was completely different from any other country in Africa. It has a very small population—fewer than two million people, which seems even smaller when you realize that there are four times as many just in New York City. It's on the west coast of the continent, just northwest of South Africa. Most of the country is desert, very hot, dry, and arid. Not many tourists make the trip. Its one claim to fame is that it has the tallest sand dunes in the world. That was enough for me.

I arrived in the capital, Windhoek, on Christmas Day. Windhoek means "corner of the wind" in Afrikaans, and it's one of the best-kept, cleanest cities I have ever seen. I stayed at the Heinitzburg Hotel, an improbable crenellated castle built by a German count for his fiancée in 1914. I had a lovely Christmas dinner and the next morning boarded a charter flight to fly north to the Kunene region. (The only way you can get to these remote places is by chartering a plane.) After three and a half hours in a small, propeller plane, I was glued to the window, desperately searching the landscape for any signs of life. Where was the airport? But there was no airport. We landed on a stretch of gravel in the middle of nowhere. A Land Rover was waiting, and a couple got out and climbed into the plane as I got out and climbed into the Land Rover. Then we drove for a good forty-five minutes through the desert. All you could see in any direction was sand. Hills and valleys of sand. I was expecting that, yet I was not ready for the desolation and the vastness. There's nothing out there. But then I got over my shock and started to differentiate a shape here and there—a tree, a bit of scrub, a pile of rocks. Gradually,

you realize that there is more to the landscape than you initially thought.

The sky was a blazingly bright blue. Not a cloud in sight—which was actually not good, according to my guide. Why? Apparently you need a few clouds in order to get the truly magnificent sunsets. So now I was scanning the sky, hoping for clouds. Finally we arrived at the Serra Cafema camp, which is built on the bank of the Kunene River. Usually when I travel, the accommodations are primitive, but this was utterly luxurious. I had my own thatched-roof bungalow, handsomely constructed of wood and canvas, with a living area and a sleeping area and a bathroom with a wonderful shower. A ceiling fan circled lazily overhead, and the coverlet on the bed was made of soft chenille. Best of all, the rooms were open to the river so you never felt confined. I could hear the rush of the rapids downstream as I fell asleep.

The next morning, we went out in the Land Rover to visit the Himba tribe, a nomadic people who wander with their cattle and goats from one watering hole to another. The women are accustomed to visitors from the camp, and they laid out handwoven baskets and

little carvings of animals to sell. But I couldn't take my eyes off their skin. To protect it from the sun, they rub a mixture of mud and animal fat all over their bodies and even into their hair, which they braid into stiff, surreal shapes. So the hair blends into the skin and the skin blends into the earth. The girls are a vision in rich reddish-brown. The clothing they wear may start out a certain color, but it all ends up looking like mud. Suddenly, I found myself thinking of a living room. How would it look if I did it all in reddish-brown? But the trick is that it can't all be the same reddish-brown. That's the mistake people make—they try to match everything perfectly. It's much more interesting when you have all these different tones of the same color, as you have here, in nature.

The Himba people live in rounded huts made out of a framework of branches spread with mud mixed with cow dung and draped in animal hides. I watched young girls milking cows, preparing food, carrying water. The women seem to do all the work while the men just sit there. They stare at you, you stare at them, and I wonder, whose life—theirs or mine—is actually weirder? I bought a little container

made of bone and leather from one girl. Her hair was amazing: it looked like the bullion fringe on a sofa, and then it was topped by these crests of mud, which reminded me of the coxcomb on a rooster.

At sunset, the guide drove to the top of a mountain where a table was waiting, laden with wine and cheese, figs, dates, and nuts. I thought of the effort it must take to bring all these provisions in, because there is nothing to be had nearby. I sat and sipped chilled Chardonnay and gazed at the mountains and the sea of sand as the sun went down. Then we headed back to camp. The heat is intense during the day, and it was a pleasure to step into the shower and put on fresh clothes before walking over to the lodge for dinner. Each night the menu was different, featuring buck or antelope or fish.

On the second day, we went out on a flat-bottomed boat to explore the river. Crocodiles, some a good eight feet long, were sunning themselves on the banks as we floated past. We stopped for lunch and stepped off the boat to eat on top of a sand dune. I finished quickly and sauntered back down, heading toward the edge of the water. "Don't do that," the

guide called. "The crocodiles can jump right out and grab you." I moved back so quickly I must have been just a blur, like a cartoon figure.

The next day, I was scheduled for what would be one of the highlights of my stay, according to the owners of the camp. A guide and I would each get on a quad bike and ride into the mountains. I may be adventuresome but I am also clumsy, and I was a little apprehensive when I saw this bike. Basically, it's an all-terrain motorcycle with four huge wheels. I was handed a helmet and we started off. The guide was using a dry riverbed as a road. I had to admit it did feel good—instead of being enclosed in a Land Rover, I was right in the midst of nature and could hear the whistle of the wind. Every once in a while, when I hit a bump, my stomach came up to my throat. But by the second hour I was feeling very comfortable and even getting a bit cocky, standing up like a champion as I zoomed along.

On the last leg of the trip, as we were heading back to camp, we came to a very steep hill. The guide said, "Go down very slowly and keep your foot on the brakes." He went first. Then it was my turn. But for some reason my brakes didn't work. In a matter of seconds, I was careening down this hill at breakneck speed, leaving the guide in the dust. It was so quick I didn't even have time for my life to flash before my eyes. The next thing I remember is the bike slamming into this large rock. The bike went flying in one direction and I went flying in another. I hit the ground face-first and my helmet flew off, because of course I had not bothered to buckle it properly. I lay there silently for a moment and my first thought was, Oh no, I've broken my nose. Blood was dripping down the side of my face, and I realized my arm was hurting. The guide radioed back to camp for help, but they couldn't get a jeep out to where we were. So I had to get back on a bike, this time sitting behind the guide, for the ride to camp. My bike was totaled. And worst of all, I had no one to blame but myself. Just as I was about to go down the hill, I had put the bike in neutral, thinking that would keep it very slow. What I didn't know was that in neutral, the brakes don't work.

Back in my bungalow, I lay down with bags of ice on my face, which was starting to swell up. My arm was swollen as well. It later turned out I had not

broken my nose but I had fractured my arm. I also had a torn retina and a concussion. I was in pain, but I was even more mad at myself. Frankly, I was lucky to be merely bashed up, considering I could have been dead or paralyzed. And once I came to this conclusion, I got out of bed, figuring, Hey, I'm here now, and I may never be here again. When you're traveling, you have to be a trouper. I didn't want to miss a thing, so I climbed into the Land Rover for the afternoon excursion. We headed off to an area where the sand dunes are marked by undulating ridges, one after the other, created by the wind. It was a mesmerizing sight, and I was glad I had roused myself.

The next camp, Damaraland, was another charter flight away. I got there just in time for a daylong trek in another Land Rover, searching for wildlife. From the beginning, I knew that I did not want to spend every day looking at animals. I'm more interested in people and local culture. Besides, after I've seen one ostrich, I'm not really that interested in the fourth and the fifth unless I see them broiled on a plate. What can I say? I'm a New Yorker. I bore easily. And this is not like the Serengeti, where you suddenly see a thousand water oxen crossing the plain. That's thrilling. Here, in this desert, things are a little quieter.

But there was one beast I was curious to see—the desert elephant. How could they survive with so little water and food? The guide explained that they are nomads, too, like the natives, and not that easy to find. But he was a great tracker and knew exactly where to look and what to look for. He showed me how to identify various kinds of dung, and to note by the dryness how long it had been there. And footprints—if they were deep, that meant they were recent enough that the sand had not started to refill them. Even something I would normally not have noticed, like a broken branch, had significance. Were the leaves green? If so, the animal that broke it could still be nearby.

As we drove off on the hunt, we spotted springboks and an oryx and more ostriches, but no elephants. I liked watching the springboks, who hop, kind of like kangaroos, as they take off on a run. We were driving in a dry riverbed and stopped in the shade of an enormous rock for lunch. After hours of tracking, I was willing to call it quits, but then the guide spotted some fresh footprints in the riverbed, and we followed them until we found the herd, complete with several babies and a few adolescents. The males can be aggressive when the females are in heat, so you don't want to get in their way. We stayed safely inside the Land Rover and kept very still when one of the bull elephants came right up to it and stuck his trunk inside to sniff all of us.

Then it was back to the Damaraland camp, which was beautifully designed to blend into the surroundings —all bleached wood, pale stucco walls, and cream-colored tents. We gathered for dinner in the open-air lounge and sat in director's chairs at a long, rough wood table. It was simple and luxurious. Drinks were always waiting as soon as I stepped out of the jeep.

The next morning I got on another small plane for the flight to the Skeleton Coast, in the northern-most stretch of the Namib Desert, one of the oldest deserts on earth. Sand blows in from the Kalahari and forms huge dunes, which are gradually encroaching on the Atlantic. This area has an unusual climate— every morning, the fog rolls in for the first three or four hours of the day, as the cool air off an icy ocean

current meets the hot air from the desert, and the desert flowers bloom. I arrived on New Year's Eve, and the path to the camp was lined with votive candles. The cooks prepared an enormous barbecue for me and ten other guests, who came from Australia and Germany and Italy. Afterward we all walked out into the bush under a sky blazing with stars to listen to the local people sing and play music. It was a lovely, peaceful New Year's Eve.

In the morning, the cooks prepared a picnic so I could spend the day on the beach. I climbed up to the seat on top of the Land Rover for the hour and a half drive to the coast. As we were heading up and over the dunes, pitching forward at the top, I started to sweat. It felt a little too much like the moment just before my accident, and I had to switch to the lower seat. I was relieved when we finally arrived.

The Skeleton Coast is a surreal landscape—mile after mile of deserted beach, with here and there a whalebone sticking up out of the sand, or a rusted hull. The sea is treacherous because of that unforgiving fog, and the hulls are the remnants of old shipwrecks. I wandered along the water's edge, collecting bits of bone, seal skulls, and shark vertebrae. Beds of black seaweed shimmered when the tide went out.

The last place I visited and, for me, the best was Sossusvlei. I spent two days there, from sunrise to sunset, just walking and taking photographs. This is where you find the famous sand dunes, the largest in the world. Some are over a thousand feet high, which is the equivalent of a hundred-story building. You just stand there in awe. Everywhere you look are these enormous mounds of sand, sinuously shaped by the wind. They reminded me of Henry Moore sculptures. They look like many things, but they do not look real. At certain times, they even seem to be moving because the wind makes ripples in the sand, continuously reshaping the top layer.

Sossusvlei is part of a large national park, and you want to get there when the sun is just coming up, to watch the color gradually seep into the landscape. As the day goes on and the sun becomes relentless, the colors change. The sand on one flank of a dune will be a completely different shade from the sand on another, because of the way the light hits it. On my last day, I was hiking through a dry lake bed and there, in the middle of nowhere, were some dead tree trunks. There was something so elemental and primitive about them, standing stark against the sand and the cobalt blue sky. A single black crow was flitting from one trunk to another, and I kept running after it, trying to photograph it. It was the only other living thing I saw. My mind was completely quiet, absorbing everything.

Everybody who comes here takes pictures, and I was trying to find the thing that would make mine different. The wood on the trees looked as if it had been sandblasted, which made sense. I started to look for patterns and tonalities. The shadows kept moving, and I was watching to see how the shadows of the larger dunes played on the smaller ones. And then I noticed these little tufts of grass, which gave the dunes a fuzz. All I could hear was the wind. The rest was silence.

As I was leaving the park, the sky turned into a technicolor extravaganza of rose and apricot and pink, and suddenly I understood what people meant when they talked about the incredible Namibian sunsets. All the colors were reflected in the dunes, and the sand looked like silk. It was almost iridescent. The sheer beauty of the place overcame me.

All I had seen before was the austerity—the sand, the rocks, the relentless heat. Now I could see beyond to the smaller details—how the fuzz of grass brings a softness to the dunes, how light plays with the color of the sand. I'm aiming for the same kind of subtlety in my work. At first, you may walk into one of my rooms and think it's very minimal. I'm always trying to say more with less, and traveling to a place like Namibia makes the point very clear. Here is a landscape that has been reduced to its essence. Simplicity is powerful. You need to hone the selection process and limit the amount of things in a space. More does not always mean better. All I want is one big stroke, like dark wood furniture against pure white walls. But it turns out that the small strokes are just as important. You may not see them immediately, but you feel them. Subliminally, you sense the softness of a fabric and the roughness of a wooden table. There's enough contrast and variation to create depth. Everything is not taken in at first glance. The room gradually reveals itself, like a flower opening in the early morning fog on the Namib Desert.

SIMPLIFY

BEFORE & AFTER

You really get to know your clients when you design something as personal as a house. When a client walks through your door a second time, you have the advantage of hindsight and familiarity.

I had worked with Alan, a bachelor, on a 1960s house in the Hamptons. It had gone through four additions and suffered from multiple personality disorder; it needed to be edited down to a single clear point of view. With the help of my associate David Rogal, I tore the whole place up and created a more casual, loftlike interior. Alan is a stockbroker, and the renovation suited his lifestyle. An astute client, he took pleasure in educating himself so he could participate in the design and construction process. He even learned to read plans.

Several years later Alan reappeared, this time with a classic apartment in a prewar building in Greenwich Village. Although it had good bones, it was predictable and boxy and needed to be updated and refreshed. It wasn't at all the kind of space we had created for him before, but he was transitioning out of that persona. He still liked a loft's open quality, but he was beginning to appreciate the formality of separate rooms. I understood he was tired of the bachelor life and wanted a place that could become a home for a couple. He was nesting, and needed some help.

The building was charming and genteel in a 1910s way, with a black-and-white-checkered marble lobby and only three apartments per floor. It was located in a traditional neighborhood of brownstones and tree-lined streets near Washington Square, a storied district that is as New York as you can get. The apartment itself was a real estate agent's dream, with a working fireplace, high ceilings, and big rooms, all with southern exposures. The rooms had a nice scale. You felt good in the spaces.

The original layout was intact, and the plan had a sense of formality and procession. The entry foyer led to a large living room. I have walked into similar places that immediately felt stuffy and uncomfortable. Yet this apartment, with big windows and lots of light, was gracious and welcoming, with great vibes and an old-fashioned, settled quality. But old is not necessarily good, and disadvantages came along with the character. The large master bedroom was off the living room and not off a hall, which was unusual.

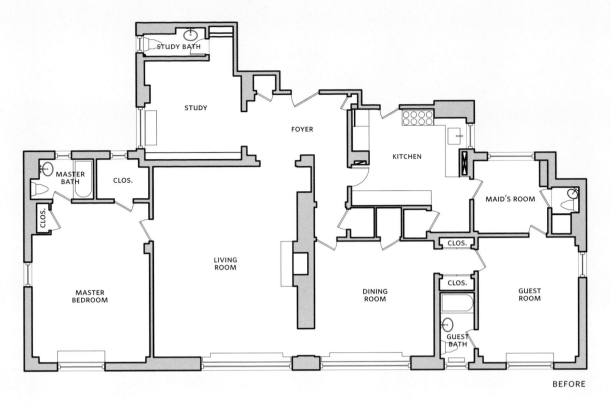

STUDY BATH

STUDY

FOYER

KITCHEN

MASTER BATH

CLOS.

CLOS.

MAID'S ROOM

LIVING ROOM

CLOS.

DINING ROOM

CLOS.

GUEST ROOM

MASTER BEDROOM

GUEST BATH

BEFORE

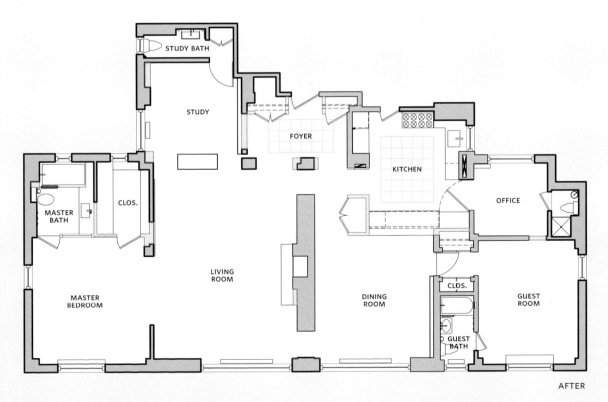

STUDY BATH

STUDY

FOYER

KITCHEN

MASTER BATH

CLOS.

OFFICE

LIVING ROOM

CLOS.

DINING ROOM

GUEST ROOM

MASTER BEDROOM

GUEST BATH

AFTER

There was a study off the entry, and a maid's room and bath next to the kitchen. To get to the guest bedroom, you had to go through the dining room. The floor plan was a little funky because of the way the bedrooms ringed the public spaces. In the living room, you were immediately aware that a door opened to the master bedroom. There was no buffer between public and private.

Most of the problems in the apartment were inherited from a different era. There was no sense of connection between rooms. The bathrooms and closets were small, and the kitchen—which was the maid's precinct when the apartment was built— was isolated from the main rooms and wouldn't allow guests to gather there. The small maid's room off the kitchen was in a back corner, as vestigial as an appendix, and had nothing to do with the main apartment. The apartment had no interior vistas, no view from one room to another. Doors didn't align. There was no sense of generosity, no expansiveness. The little arched doorways were quaint, but they had no impact on the space.

Details in a distinguished old apartment can play a strong supporting role, but the moldings here were thin and matter-of-fact. The herringbone floors, which I always find disappointingly safe and conventional, were worn out. For once, I wouldn't have to beg the client to let us replace them.

When I look at a space I'm designing, I don't focus as much on the positives as on the negatives. I study the disadvantages, because correcting what's wrong often launches the design concept. In this case, there were big and little things that had to be corrected, from the floor plan to the detail. My job was to make a new whole out of the apartment while at the same time subtly tweaking its character. Alan liked the comfort of rooms, but he was still fond of the freedom of lofts. I was the diplomat negotiating between the two types of contradictory space. We all wanted to retain the grace of the past. But how to make it work for a contemporary lifestyle without making it look strictly contemporary? I decided to boil the existing apartment down, to simplify it and give it a fresh point of view. As in cooking, reducing makes things stronger. We'd take it down to its essence.

My immediate goal was to find a way to open up the apartment while still keeping a sense of designated spaces with specific uses, like the foyer, living room, and bedrooms. We performed surgery on the plan, creating passages between rooms that would open them to each other. This was a selective renovation, and by limiting the surgery, we maintained the character as we contained the costs. The idea was to make the maximum impact with the minimum amount of structural work. You don't have to do a gut renovation to transform an apartment. You can accomplish the same results by being strategic and limiting the scope. Surprisingly, only three or four incisions were necessary to open up Alan's space: we cut only when it counted.

The living room was already a nice size, but I felt that by making it look bigger, we could give more impact to the apartment. I started at the front door, closing the doorway between the study and foyer and opening the wall shared by the study and living room. That firmed up the foyer as the introduction to the apartment and expanded the depth of the living room by the depth of the study. I put a double-sided, see-through wall cabinet where the wall of the study had been, like a pass-through, to keep the study defined as a separate space. It acts as an architectural divider between the two rooms. Your eye always finds the farthest point in a room, so it looks past the shelves and stops at the back wall. The study is still the study, but now the living room seems twelve feet longer.

I continued the surgery in the living room by cutting out a short segment of the fireplace wall to open it up to the dining room. With the two openings, what had been compartmentalized rooms became more porous. I did the same between the kitchen and dining room, so that the two rooms, which were closed off by a door and closet, opened to each other. No one working in the kitchen now is isolated from the guests. It's friendlier.

BEFORE: VIEW FROM FOYER

When I'm doing a job, I can't wait for the day when the construction phase is over and I can finally look at the space, empty and pristine. It's one of the best moments of any project. There's nothing else to distract you or to depend on—just the bare bones.

BEFORE: LIVING ROOM

CONSTRUCTION: LIVING ROOM

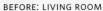

THE BIGGEST TRANSFORMATION was between the living room and the master bedroom, where there was that awkward little door. This is where the trust that Alan and David and I had built up in the Hamptons renovation worked in favor of the new design.

Many people feel that a good idea requires a lot of work to develop. Yes, sometimes it does. But when you're in a relaxed situation with good client rapport, the wheels turn very fast and you have the freedom to let your instincts run free. In the Hamptons, Alan had learned to expect and respond to creative thinking. Coming from Wall Street, his wheels turn in a different direction, but because of our experience he's grown to respect solutions that come spontaneously. So I felt comfortable throwing an idea out there, and the idea in question addressed that living room/master bedroom door: why not just open up the wall really wide?

This was my thinking: the bedroom shares the southern wall with the living room, and if the divider between them could open to offer a view of the big bedroom window, it would really widen and brighten the whole living space. You'd see the full length of the wall from the living room, and it would be two rooms wide. Then you could put in a big sliding door that would let you close the bedroom up.

I first showed Alan the plans with the door closed, and then I told him what I wanted to do. I was trying to anticipate his objections once he knew that the dividing wall could disappear. Some people would have balked at the idea, assuming they weren't going to have a bedroom anymore. But Alan heard me out. He realized that the bedroom door would just become a really big bedroom door. He could process the thought. A new client might not take that chance.

So I created a nine-foot opening between the master bedroom and living room. Now when you walk into the living room, you feel like the space goes all the way into the master bedroom. Instead of isolated windows, each in its own room, you have an expansive run of windows from the dining room through the living room to the bedroom.

The nine-foot-wide sliding door works like a moving wall. We even hung a painting on it, so wherever it is, it looks like a wall, not a door. The living room is still a living room, but it has annexed all the adjacent space, so it seems huge. The space flows. The Japanese have made an art out of "borrowing" views from the larger landscape to increase the apparent size of a garden. Here we borrowed space from adjacent rooms and gave the apartment a larger scale. We established continuity between the two spaces by carrying fabrics and finishes from the living room into the bedroom. We gave Alan the best of both worlds, the sense of a loft and the proprieties of a gracious apartment built of discrete rooms.

THE BIG DECISIONS helped me make the smaller ones. The lighter, roomier environment that was emerging needed to be reinforced by everything from details to materials. To let the rooms in the new configuration relate to each other, we had to simplify. Each room had to glide into the other without interference; the spaces had to agree in order to merge. The details and materials were the threads that connected rooms together.

Simplification started with cleaning up the old apartment, removing details that didn't contribute to the new whole. Many of the doorways had meaningless arches, which we either straightened out or eliminated. The new straight lines were minimal and clean. We simplified the moldings, eliminating trim from the doorways altogether. We didn't want the eye traveling down to the baseboard. The ceiling, crossed with structural beams, never had any moldings, and we kept the beams clean, to complement the unadorned walls. The existing baseboards were weak, so we removed them and installed flat baseboards that hinted at tradition without being fussy or pretentious. They were neat enough to turn corners, and to disappear where they didn't. On the new walls, we didn't use the baseboards at all, and the undecorated planes inched the apartment toward abstraction.

Simplicity is effortless, uncomplicated. When I'm doing a room, I try not to overthink it. I want it to feel as if everything is where it was meant to be.

BEFORE: LIVING ROOM

CONSTRUCTION: LIVING ROOM

THE EXISTING MANTEL was original but undistinguished, and its moldings and arched opening made it inappropriate for the new apartment. Nothing could be done about the fireplace's very small opening, so we started to think about how to take that and make it into a much bolder statement. We always paint the inside of the firebox black because I think it makes it disappear, and by surrounding the opening with black slate and mitering its corners into a forced perspective, the firebox seemed to expand and become larger. It was a subtle detail, next to not there, but it had a significant spatial effect.

The slate surround, which I topped with a flat-screen TV, compensates for the fact that we did not have furniture centered in front of the fireplace. The visual weight of the fireplace anchors the room. Symmetry is not necessary for balance, and it can freeze a room. I think you can find a balance in asymmetry that is more subtle and intriguing. A subliminal order can give a natural ease to a space. It doesn't hit you over the head with the obvious.

RENDERING: LIVING ROOM

My kind of simplicity is actually very complex.
It's a bit like a choir, with all the voices singing
different parts. Yet when you hear them,
they sound like one voice. The separate elements
blend in perfect harmony.

BENJAMIN MOORE
BLACK PEPPER
2130-40

BENJAMIN MOORE
SEASIDE SAND
2110-40

WE IMPORTED THE SAME INFORMALITY to the kitchen. I took down the wall separating the kitchen from the dining room and built a countertop between the rooms for guests who want to pull up a stool and hang out over a glass of wine, watching Alan cook. You still have a dining room, but now the rooms can accommodate the more relaxed lifestyle that we've set up in the rest of the apartment. The change was straightforward, but it completely transformed the apartment's attitude. Now the formal spaces could be used informally. By simply eliminating a couple of doors—the one into the kitchen and another into the dining room—we unboxed the rooms and connected the spaces. We saved some money by putting existing cabinets under the counter, and then had some fun with the pantry. There was a maid's room at the end of the kitchen, which we remodeled as a home office. I used the same pivot door to close the office and the pantry. When you open the pantry, you close the office, and when you open the office, you close the pantry.

A finished room may look simple, but it isn't simple to do. Some elements, seen individually, may seem so simple they are almost nondescript, but when all the pieces are put together they create a sense of warmth and unity.

BEFORE: MASTER BEDROOM

CONSTRUCTION: MASTER BEDROOM AND BATHROOM

THE SMALL BATHROOMS AND CLOSETS that you often see in prewar apartments are not among their charms. I found a way to enlarge the master bath by robbing Peter to pay Paul. Because the bedroom borrowed space visually from the living room, thanks to the widened opening, I could subtract space from the bedroom and add it to the master bath and closet.

I had two ways of expanding the bathroom. The first was illusion. We did the bathroom walls in frosted mirror that was not fully reflective—the cloudiness softened the effect of walls as boundaries. Then we did the floors in stainless-steel tile to add another reflective quality that made the limits of the space ambiguous. We also frosted the small window to soften the light (and to give privacy). To gain more light, we installed a marble patterned window from India, which dissolved the wall and transmitted southern light into the bath. It also contributed a little romance.

Beyond illusion, we expanded the bathroom physically, but it was touchy. In New York apartment buildings, there are rules prohibiting wet spaces over dry: you don't want to put a toilet over somebody's bedroom. So we couldn't move the fixtures. But we did move the front wall of the bathroom forward into the bedroom by four feet. That gave us a bigger bathroom without violating the rules. The move also increased the length of the adjacent closet by four feet. The added advantage was that instead of keeping the bedroom rectangular, the expanded bath and closet squared the bedroom and created a more pleasant proportion.

To balance the closet and bathroom doors, I added a third dummy door on the same wall. Now the whole elevation is unified around the translucent window into the bath. Instead of doing flush doors, I created raised panels, a nice 1940s-style architectural focal point that framed the bed.

RENDERING: DINING ROOM

FABRICS: DINING ROOM

I don't tie a room to any particular look
or period. I put together a mix of furniture,
with some simple pieces and others
that are more elaborate in their design.
I like a mix. It keeps you intrigued.

I DESIGNED ALAN'S APARTMENT after a trip to Borneo, where I floated down rivers on a houseboat. The colors for the walls and floors came from that experience. I would lie back in a chair out on the deck and stare up at the grays and blues and whites of the sky, framed by the browns of tree trunks (with snakes coiled in their branches) leaning over the water. It was a beautiful, strong palette, and I thought it suited Alan.

I started by painting the walls and the ceilings white, to give a traditional apartment a more modern feel and to play up the architecture. We smoothed all the walls and sharpened every corner to give the space a crispness. The walls started to look geometric. A satin finish on the ceilings created reflections that made them feel taller and doubled the impact of the light from the windows. In New York, you're always trying to stretch that tight spatial sandwich between floor and ceiling any way you can.

Dark floors throughout the apartment help the flow, and the sheen of the floors and the darkness give the space depth. But I didn't want the floors in this prewar apartment to look brand spanking new, so we invented an aging process to make them seem worn. First, we bleached the wood to make it lighter. Next, we rubbed in an ebony stain and then wiped it off, so the higher surfaces went light and the lower ones stayed dark. It gave the floor layers, like strata, which convey a sense of age and history.

I like to use area rugs to anchor my furniture groupings. I chose a jute, banana fiber, and wool rug for the living room, and then used the same material in the master bedroom as an insert within a slate-gray wall-to-wall carpet. The slate-gray carpet reappears in the study and refers back to the mantelpiece. When you repeat an element, you want to use it in a slightly different way each time. Then you get a subliminal sense of continuity without monotony.

In the kitchen and the foyer, I made virtual area rugs by inserting beige limestone into the floor. First we laid plywood so that the limestone tile would come flush with the surrounding wood floor. We trimmed the insert with a strip of satin stainless steel, just an eighth of an inch thick, to delineate the change in materials.

Having opened up the apartment, I didn't want to close it down again with a predictable furniture plan. With the study and the bedroom opening onto the living room, we set up an unconventional way of thinking about a space. You can't just push all the furniture up against walls that have been eroded. You start to float the furniture in space. Then the rugs or the stone inserts in the floor become islands within that space, and you move from one to another as you move through the rooms. Kyoto's rock gardens, where stones are floating in a sea of white pebbles, use the same concept to express tranquility and serenity. My furniture islands float in the context of the same color wrapping the ceilings and walls.

To give the apartment a sense of continuity, I used the same materials throughout all the rooms—a blue-gray bouclé, a taupe polished wool, and a tan leather. For me, different fabrics in different rooms is the fussy route. Using the same fabrics is another way of simplifying. Visually, you have continuity throughout the whole space since you see from room to room, yet the different uses give each space individuality. Repeating the fabrics helps erase the separation between the living room and bedroom. You don't think of fabrics as having a spatial consequence, but they do. I used floor-to-ceiling curtains in the living room and the bedroom; with the bedroom door open, you have a sense that the curtains and therefore the windows continue across the wall. A gauzy scrim underneath the curtains cuts glare but still allows you to see the view. That reduces the contrast of light between outside and inside, creating a softer, more atmospheric interior. I back these up with blackout shades in the bedroom for when you really want the room dark.

FABRICS: LIVING ROOM AND MASTER BEDROOM

Most people have tunnel vision when it comes to picking fabric. They see something and say, Oh, that's pretty! Wouldn't it be nice on the wing chair? But they're not thinking of what it will do to the room as a whole.

———————

When you're picking out fabric, bunch your samples together and see how harmonious they are. Add another. Does that make the combination stronger? At one point, they will stop supporting each other and start to compete.

WITHIN THE CONTINUITY, we mixed the furniture by shape and style to create variety. I like to use pieces from different countries and periods so they comment on each other visually and culturally. There's a primitive bed from Borneo in the study—a daybed made out of ironwood, done in Dutch Colonial style by a Dutch architect working at the turn of the century for one of the regional sultans. A little history gives a different dimension to a room. Next to it is Warren Platner's 1960s wire-frame chair. Both have strong lines but bring totally different connotations. In the bedroom, I nested a white Parsons side table beneath a traditional console. They talk to each other. To mask an off-balance window, I designed a delicate metal floor-to-ceiling étagère. Backlit, it creates a strong silhouette that changes the subject, so you don't stop to wonder why that one odd window is there.

Sometimes I will use the same fabrics all through an apartment. Is that boring? No. The same fabric will look different under each light and in each situation.

I've learned that an empty room can work perfectly well.
If the architecture is strong and balanced, it is already
giving you the emotion of the space. It may not need much
to make it work even better.

CONSTRUCTION: DINING ROOM AND KITCHEN

CONSTRUCTION: DINING ROOM AND KITCHEN

APARTMENTS OF THIS VINTAGE usually had overhead light in the middle of a room, but a century later, we're much more sophisticated about lighting, especially since the miniaturization of the light bulb. I find that light from a centrally placed fixture is often harsh and obvious, and it centers a room that you don't necessarily want to have a center, especially if you want space to flow. The wrong lighting can kill a space, and it can be very unflattering to the people in it.

Here, I went to great lengths to keep the walls simple and abstract, the better to set off furniture and people. This is the principle behind all galleries and most museum spaces. I kept the ceiling "clean" for the same reason, leaving the beams exposed as an architectural feature.

But you still need ambient light. Because the ceilings were concrete, I couldn't recess lights, and I didn't want to drop the ceiling to hide them—I'd lose the beams, not to mention precious height. That would horizontalize a space whose generosity lies in the vertical dimension. So for the dining room, living room, and master bedroom, I found very inconspic-

uous halogen lighting that you clip on wires. Because the fixtures are low voltage, you have to find a place to put the transformer—preferably hidden outside the immediate area. This is a far better alternative to traditional track lighting, which can be clumsy. We used adjustable fixtures so we could play with the lights and direct them exactly where we wanted. The halogens updated the apartment by bringing a gallery-like feeling to the space. The miniature bulbs are discreet and minimal, simply suspended on a line. You hardly know they're there. Yet trained on the perimeter of the space, they bounce off walls and light the room gently.

My islands of furniture float in that environment of luminous walls and surfaces, and within the islands I positioned table and floor lamps to create pools of light. They help define a sense of place and punctuate the ambient light with spots of intensity. I like to mix different types of lighting. I'll even use the occasional chandelier. It gives you a more specific light within the general, and you need both.

I like to float furniture in a
room. When chairs and sofas are
not tethered to the walls,
it creates a sense of more space.
The room feels boundless.

WHEN I PRESENT a finished project to a client, I
normally walk them through with all the doors open.
But with Alan, I closed every door because I wanted
him to discover each space. When he got to the
master bedroom, he slid open the door and immediately understood it: "Wow, I can lie in bed and watch
TV, and still see the fire burning in the living room."
The gracious prewar apartment could also function
like one big loft.

It's hard for any client to absorb everything at
once. Alan is very methodical. For him, walking
through with us was one thing, but being in the
apartment, alone and with friends, and actually using
it was another. It turns out that he likes to keep the
door to the bedroom open, even when he entertains.
There was no reason to close it once he saw how well
the bedroom flowed visually into the rest of the
apartment. It was the best of both worlds.

When I look at the completed job, I feel that the
gestures that really make it work are the expanded
fireplace, the opening into the master bedroom, and
the new vistas from room to room. There is no sense
that this is a bachelor pad. It is a home. It represented
the union of the client's desires and our abilities to
realize his expectations for the space.

OBVIOUSLY, IT WORKED. Seven months later he was
married.

RENDERING: MASTER BEDROOM

SIMPLIFY

ENVIRONMENTS

I FELT LIKE MOSES WHEN I DIVIDED THE LIVING ROOM of this Hamptons beach house in two. The first thing you see when you walk inside the house is space. It feels light and airy. The living room was wide and split by a natural axis that ended in French doors opening to the garden and a pool. I could see what the room wanted to be and planned two furniture groups with enough seats for lots of guests.

An eighteenth-century English chair, a Chinese drop-leaf table, a Bertoia wire-frame chair, and a Saarinen table all freely orbit a big, one-armed, high-backed ratchet sofa on the left side of the room. Usually a fireplace gathers furniture like a magnet, but this time I arranged things a little differently—I made it part of the background. I'm always trying to find subliminal ways to give spaces a different twist, to break rules and tweak convention. Sofas and chairs don't have to face the fireplace.

But it's still a focal point, and I like to do something interesting on the mantel. Here, a Mapplethorpe photo spars with an antique Philippine wood wheel—a square next to a circle. The different geometries balance each other out. Normally you would expect to see a mirror centered over the fireplace, but instead I hung to one side a nineteenth-century mirror from Syria, inlaid with mother-of-pearl. The scale is big enough to balance the French doors to the right of the fireplace, and now the fireplace is flanked with light on both sides. The low console under the mirror, which can also be used

as a bar, is something I designed. Steel legs support a slab of rough-edged wood.

There's more mirror on the right side of the room, but there it's used very differently. Three long horizontal bands of mirror wrap a corner and echo the lines of a corner banquette. It's my own version of something I once saw in Sweden. It gives you fractured glimpses of the room, which adds animation. Mirrors connect both sides of the room, but in a dynamic way. You don't see the entire space as you enter but discover elements in reflections.

The consistently neutral colors also unify the room. I repeated fabrics—natural linen, creamy wool—across the aisle, and each side has its own Bertoia chair. On the wall opposite the fireplace, I draped a table to continue the line and volume of the banquette. An architectural model of a wood steeple is lit from the inside to project light and shadow on the white walls. The two furniture groups sit on one large sisal carpet, which pulls the whole together and adds a casual touch to the dark wood floor.

When I'm designing, I'll pull together a mix of period and contemporary furnishings. Then I start to eliminate. Does the room still work without this piece? If so, get rid of it. When you do that, the space becomes much stronger. It's as if you've boiled it down to its essence.

WHEN I WAS ASKED TO DESIGN THE INTERIORS AT 15 Union Square West, I was intrigued to learn that the building was originally designed in the 1870s as the Tiffany & Co. store. The residential conversion added a new glass facade and a wide-open floor plan. As soon as you enter the main area—which serves as living room, dining room, and kitchen— I wanted your eye to go to the farthest point. That dictated the furniture plan, which started with a sofa designed as one big eye-catching curve in the far corner. That's also where you would logically want to sit, because that area gets the most light. The back of the sofa is higher than normal to give you a sense of containment, which is helpful in a room where the ceiling is eighteen feet high. It's a dramatic space, and I was playing against the rectangular room and the rectangular windows by arranging the seating in a circle.

The dining table, which acts as the central focal point, is also a circle. I didn't want to do a conventional set of dining chairs, so I mixed traditional Chinese with midcentury modern. There are other intriguing juxtapositions in the seating area, where a Burmese drum and a Syrian chest serve as end tables in a group that includes an Ethiopian chief's chair. A weather-beaten farm trough from Indonesia stands on a pedestal behind the sofa and looks almost like a piece of sculpture. It's a rough, gnarly contrast to the clean contemporary lines you see almost everywhere else.

Since the kitchen is exposed, I wanted it to feel like fine cabinetry so it would blend smoothly into the room. The cabinet doors have panels of wood or frosted glass framed in bronze, which echoes the bronze frames on the strikingly tall windows. I wasn't trying to hide the kitchen— I just wanted to give it a strong aesthetic so it could hold its own in a very large space.

It would have been a little ridiculous to run cabinets all the way up to that ceiling. Instead, I built niches into the upper portion of the wall and lined them with LED lights, which can be programmed in different colors. It's like an art installation, and it gives the whole room a glow. Large white lampshades hang over the island and bring your eye back down to a more human scale.

THE ENTRY TO THIS CHARMING HAMPTONS COTTAGE was a little abrupt. The front door opened smack into the living room, killing any intimacy and baring everything at once. There was no drama of discovery. But I don't think the only alternative to this condition, which is very common, is a formal foyer enclosed by walls. We invented a solution based on the idea that peeking into the space might be a good approach.

First, we conjured up the notion of an entry by painting a black "rug," with glossy outdoor deck paint, on the white floor. I suppose I could have bought a real rug, but that would have been too literal. I was creating a virtual foyer, and I wanted to simplify the thought down to its essence. A French iron pedestal table—made around the same time as the Eiffel Tower, when craftsmen were translating classic forms into industrial materials—provides a place to park your bag. Second, I placed a black, gridded Chinese folding screen to the left. The screen allows glimpses into the living room. Once you reach the pedestal table on the black carpet, you turn left and enter the main space. The cottage was suddenly more polite. We subtracted the space of the virtual entry from the living room, and added etiquette.

The cue for the black carpet was the black handrail. The black gave the white space a welcome sense of depth and self-assuredness. The contrast was graphic and modern, and the neutral black and white brought out the sculptural qualities of the iron table, which I had cherished and held onto for a long time. I give up unique pieces like this only when they go for a good cause—and a good client.

When you round the corner past the Chinese screen, you arrive in a small living room that looks boundless because of the white. I took care to keep it sparsely populated—an Eero Saarinen chair, a French 1940s chair, and a roomy high-backed ratchet sofa that I designed with one splayed arm (two arms would have closed it off as you came in). All you need really is a few good pieces, and each of these holds your eye. The all-white background helped reduce the visual competition. Since the furniture has a strong linear quality, I wanted an irregular shape on the floor. The free-form cowhide makes the room feel a little loose, and the color worked with the beige leather on the French chair, the linen on the sofa, and the darker linen on the Saarinen chair. I hung an Edward Weston photograph on the screen because I wanted a focal point above the sofa. The screen is folded but the picture is straight and floats in front. It's a reminder of the wall that isn't really there. The Chinese screen is distantly related to the carved teak Indonesian screens over the fireplace, which were once used as transoms above doors. They give the room another contrast of dark and light—a very graphic touch.

SOMETIMES DIFFICULT ROOMS CAN TURN OUT TO BE the most successful. This bedroom had all sorts of peaks and juts with high windows and strange little alcoves. Some walls were paneled and others were not. There are designers who would try to camouflage all the different shapes with flowery wallpaper, overloading the room. But I chose to simplify things and paint the ceiling and walls the same cool bluish white—Benjamin Moore's Patriotic White. By washing the room in one color, you neutralize the boundaries. The lines between ceiling and walls blur, and there is more of a sense of cohesion. The focus is on the color, not the angles. It's more restful that way.

But there was still one problem. How do you create intimacy in such a large room? I decided to do a seating alcove by the fireplace and set it off with curtains. The tiebacks give you the sense of a small, private area within the large space. I emphasized the separation of the spaces by laying in a darker carpet by the fireplace. The carpet and the upholstery fabrics are all slight variations on the color of the walls. I'm working with small tonal shifts between light blues and grays.

I hung the photo over the fireplace asymmetrically. I think it's nice to throw one thing off in a room. It relaxes and humanizes a space. It makes it less strict and predictable. If the photo had been centered over the fireplace, you would have just registered it as part of a typical grouping. I think you actually focus on it much more this way.

I built a stainless-steel frame around the king-size bed to delineate the sleeping area and hung more fabric behind the headboard to add softness. The bed doesn't look like the rest of the furniture in the room, and the frame establishes its own zone.

There's really no reason that bedside tables have to match, and I like the imbalance created by two different pieces. If one table is higher or older or a different color, it invites a different treatment. Here each table has its own collection. By using my

favorite Hansen swing-arm lamps on the wall, I give myself more room for a tablescape. To the right of the bed, I've got a table on top of a table—a little Chinese altar table inlaid with mother-of-pearl holds six-hundred-year-old Thai porcelains, all arrayed on top of a Burmese table. And under that I've propped a photograph on the floor, which gives you something to discover in an unexpected place. The square, boxy tables in the alcove are Chinese, made of bamboo.

Soft colors evoke a sense of calm and peacefulness. Furniture floats against cool white walls.

BENJAMIN MOORE
BROOKLINE
BEIGE
HC-47

BENJAMIN MOORE
PATRIOTIC
WHITE
2135-70

BENJAMIN MOORE
NOVEMBER
SKIES
2018-50

BENJAMIN MOORE
ICED SLATE
2130-60

ORIGINALLY, THIS FRONT DOOR WAS SET IN A BAY made of brick. I knocked out the bricks and replaced them with glass to open the foyer to the light and the view. All of a sudden what had been a traditional door set into a traditional wall became a floating door flanked, on the porch outside, by two traditional columns. It was an interesting blur of old and new. In some lights, the glass vanished, giving the whole space a dreamy quality. I played on that feeling with the way I laid the floor. It starts out by the door as a classic diamond pattern, but the placement of the smaller diamonds gradually becomes more haphazard and playful.

An Ed Ruscha painting hanging over a nineteenth-century Chinese altar table offers its own comment on the door, which is lacquered black. I usually do front doors in black because I like them to stand out.

Decorating is not an equation. There's no right or wrong. We're after an emotion, and the path to it is unpredictable.

BENJAMIN MOORE
DRY SAGE
2142-40

BENJAMIN MOORE
SOFT FERN
2144-40

I USED SEVEN DIFFERENT COLORS IN THIS ROOM, although you might not realize it since they're all subtle variations on a cool, clean theme. I started with the walls, which are painted a soft sage green. Then I used a blue-gray wool for the continuous headboard. This simple element solves a common dilemma in a guest room—should you get one bed or two?—with great flexibility. The two beds can be separate or can be rolled together and turned into one king-size bed, if you like. I used the same blue-gray wool to upholster the box springs, so the beds feel more connected to the headboard.

The curtains are a pearly beige, the coverlets are cream, and the chair, from West Elm, is covered in a white stretchy fabric. When the carpet was delivered, its two pieces turned out to be from two different dye lots. It was more of a cream color by the beds and more of a sage color by the chair. But I actually didn't mind the change in tone. It created the sense that the beds were floating on a platform. It took a little bit of effort to convince the client to let it be, but I think it brings something different to the room. And it started me thinking about doing insets in carpets in other places. The point is, not every mistake is a disaster. Try to relax. It can be interesting to let chance be part of the design process.

GOOD DESIGN HAD NOTHING TO DO WITH THE CREATION of this new Nantucket house. At first I thought we'd just paint everything white and call it a day. But then I went back and looked at the living room again. I'm always searching for ways to challenge the conventional floor plan. This was a space that had an unfortunate bowling-alley quality. I found that turning the furniture on an angle really dynamized the room and literally altered the perspective. It made a narrow space seem much wider. I also took the doors off a far closet to create an alcove that helps break the box. That little space becomes a niche for a wood table and a tablescape. The eye finds it and lingers.

The group of chairs in the room resembles a session at the United Nations. All different races and creeds are represented. I like to mix pieces because it's more democratic—not just one culture, one price level, one point of view. There's an angular reading chair on a stainless-steel frame and a more traditional tufted ottoman. The subliminal message of an ottoman is to kick back and put your feet up;

this one is upholstered in vinyl, so you don't have to be afraid of messing it up. I used commercial-grade fabrics on the sofa and easy chairs, for durability.

The kitchen used to gobble up nearly half the space. But we simply eliminated a wall and confined the cupboards to the far end of the room. All of a sudden we wound up with a much bigger space. I arranged the cupboards and appliances into a composition, letting it all show. No hiding the fridge. The big table, placed between the kitchen's working wall and the living area, is ambiguous. It serves as a kitchen island as well as the dining table in the newly open space. Around it, I alternated caned chairs from Burma with curvaceous Verner Panton chairs. The fiberglass Panton chairs are easy to wipe clean.

Exposing the kitchen to the room also warmed up the space. It's a vacation house, with a deck outside. Now my clients can boil the lobsters while they're chatting with their guests. It seemed a natural, straightforward way to relax the house.

THE BEST WAY TO THINK ABOUT A ROOM IS TO START
with its function. That's also the best way to make
sure every room in a house won't look the same.
I always think a room where you watch TV should
be like a cocoon. I want my clients to feel protected
and soothed. You can paint the room dark, so it
engulfs you. Or you can achieve a nice snug effect
with gentle gradations of texture and tone. Here,
grass cloth on the walls, suede on the sofas, cowhide
on the ottoman, leather on the Arne Jacobsen chair,
and a tweedy carpet all bring a sense of comfort
to the room. The soft materials want soft light, so I
used translucent schoolhouse shades that roll up
from the bottom to filter the sun. On other windows
I swap in regular shades.

When you enter from the other rooms, which
have painted walls, you immediately feel the
difference, which is reinforced by the changeover to
a soothing palette of light browns and creams. I've
avoided sharp contrasts in favor of shifts in tone,
so the colors are not really monochromatic but
slightly varied, like a cloudy sky or the bark of trees.

To keep the subtlety from verging into
monotony, I added a large Chinese teak window
screen above the sofa, which creates shadows on the
wall and complements the rounded, more massive
shapes of the sofas and chairs. It's not a simple
grid like the windows and doors nearby. Its intriguing
internal geometries give the room a focal point to
which the eye always returns, like a visual puzzle.
I like the dialogue it sets up with Jacobsen's 1950s
Swan chair.

Why an ottoman instead of a coffee table? I
find that so many people want to live in a more
relaxed way. You can put your feet up on an ottoman,
but it's not socially correct to do that on a coffee
table. So an ottoman allows you to feel you can do
whatever you want in the space. It gives you
permission. It also gives you the flexibility of having
another seat. And it's large enough to sleep on,
which makes it even more practical.

BENJAMIN MOORE
VAN BUREN
BROWN
HC-70

BENJAMIN MOORE
BROOKLINE
BEIGE
HC-47

BENJAMIN MOORE
PLYMOUTH
BROWN
HC-73

I don't like to feel hemmed in by objects. That's why I prefer a simple environment. I want to be able to see how each furniture group is composed and notice how light spills across a floor. There should be air around each piece of furniture, so it has room to breathe. I want to feel that I can stretch out. I like the sense that everything is not set. The room can still evolve. The person living there can grow and change.

THE GREAT ASSET OF THIS LANDING WAS THAT IT WAS too small, too short, and too awkward to be used for anything much. So we could do almost anything we wanted. A landing is a traditional sort of space, especially if it's sandwiched between a spindle railing and raised panel doors, and I thought a traditional piece of furniture was appropriate. I found a painted table, probably Italian and probably nineteenth century, with boldly bowed baroque legs, like a piano's. The scale of the legs alone was irreverent. Most people would put it in a larger space, but I thought this small area needed a big gesture—there was nothing to compete with.

I floated the table on a diagonal in the middle, so it didn't belong to the surrounding walls but took on a life of its own. I leaned a full-length mirror against the wall to reflect an unseen side of the table—it's a very sculptural, three-dimensional piece, and the overall form was worth the 360-degree coverage. But I didn't pick a conventional mirror. It's a piece of stainless steel, polished and then framed with a satin finish. It acts like a mirror and expands the tight space, but there's a little distortion to the reflection, which makes it more interesting. I've done leaning mirrors for years. It's become a signature, but I'm still playing around with the idea and this is how it has evolved.

In 1970, Achille Castiglioni designed one of my favorite lamps, the Parentesi, a great mini-light that glides up and down on a vertical wire. It's flexible lighting that takes up hardly any space, which is why it was perfect for this landing. I tucked a leather ottoman beneath the table, which suggests you could actually sit there and work. The table also serves as a pedestal for a bronze sculpture from Thailand—another big gesture in a small space.

BILLY BALDWIN USED TO SAY THAT EVERY GUEST ROOM
should have wonderful linens, a good reading
light, and a desk where you could write a note. I say
they should also have a sense of individuality. Like
dining rooms and powder rooms, you're there only
for a short period of time, so you can afford a few
more theatrics. Here, I started out very simply with
a bed from Crate & Barrel and a rug made out of
brown wrapping paper. I upped the drama quotient
with an Indian desk inlaid with bone and ebony.
No one would expect to see it paired with a Verner
Panton chair, but that's why I like it. The chair is
a little tough and very sleek. But what really makes
the room is the coral paint—just on one wall.
The rest are my favorite Benjamin Moore Super
White. The coral casts a warm, flattering glow.
Then the black lamp and the black-and-white photo
propped against the wall cut the sweetness.

| BENJAMIN MOORE |
| PINK PEACH |
| 2009-40 |

| BENJAMIN MOORE |
| DAWN PINK |
| 2010-50 |

| BENJAMIN MOORE |
| DARK BEIGE |
| 2165-40 |

Simplicity is all about variations on
a theme. You choose just a few
elements and keep remaking them
over and over.

If you're open and responsive, a room
will tell you what it wants to be.
I'll always step back and look at my
work as I'm putting a room together,
and if it doesn't instinctively feel
right, I'll come back and try again.
Just don't overanalyze it.

IT'S REALLY NOT ENOUGH TO SLAP A MIRROR ON A WALL to make a small room look bigger. Often you're just trading one defect for another. Chances are it will feel cold, even soulless. Mirrors should be subtle in order to work best.

You probably didn't even notice the mirror in here at first. This small bedroom had a tall ceiling that made the proportions awkward, so I started by lowering the apparent height of the room by running an eighteen-inch-tall strip of mirror along the top of the wall. The mirror does two things: it makes you feel that the wall is a partition and the room continues beyond it, and it reflects the ceiling and seems to blend into it, making it seem to start lower. I upholstered the rest of the wall in gray mohair, which establishes a new ceiling line. I love the color of the mohair. It makes me think of cloudy skies.

A slab of stainless steel between the two windows acts as another kind of mirror, and blows out that wall entirely. You're not sure where the boundaries lie. The carpet is done in two tones—a gray taupe and a pearl gray. It's like wet and dry concrete. I had the night table made of ivory-colored parchment. It's another strong horizontal, like the bed. I hung the painting over the night table instead of the bed because there's more power in asymmetry. It's also opposite the doorway, so the painting provides a strong visual when you look in from the hall.

The room would not be as successful without the crisp white linens and lampshades. They give it a lightness of spirit.

A FOYER IS THE START OF A NARRATIVE, THE BEGINNING of a thread that carries throughout a house. Like the first notes of a song, an entry introduces the house by telling you what is going to happen, what the message will be. The setting creates a sense of drama and sets the mood.

In this house in Malibu the foyer offers various hints of what's to come. You see the play of texture—a swag of rough rope against a smooth wall. You see the strong architecture—a sweeping staircase with a white plaster railing as liquid as a Brancusi. And then you see the intriguing mix of materials on the floor—rough stone and old planks brought from Sweden and worn smooth.

I like something that catches your eye as soon as you enter a space. The table is a nineteenth-century French factory table made of iron and painted an industrial gray; it turns almost white in the sunlight pouring in through the front door. The remnants of old paint and stains on the top of the table make a wonderful contrast to the pure white walls. Every object sitting on the table, and even the painting over it, is white. Next to ghostly, these items fade into the wall, without distraction, making the table stand out even more.

From the floor and the table to the objects and that line of rope on the wall, I'm juxtaposing smooth and rough over and over again. It's the equivalent of a brushstroke or a pencil sketch—quick, suggestive, gestural. The house follows its lead.

I'm interested in color and light and shape. Pattern can be a distraction. For me, the pattern comes from the different forms and colors in the space.

THERE'S JUST SOMETHING RESTFUL ABOUT HORIZONTALS. A horizontal line reminds me of the horizon, and that moment of standing on a beach and looking out to where the water meets the sky. Modernist architects like to keep a low horizon line in their spaces. In the dining room of this traditional cottage, a long slab of cherry table cantilevered past its two industrial bases delivers that serenity in a contemporary way. A narrow horizontal slot on the back of the accompanying banquette counteracts the bulkiness of the piece and lets the light show through. Playing horizontals against verticals is a good way to animate a room. Vertical lines have more energy and balance the more tranquil horizontals. Here the table and banquette play against two vertical cabinets that frame the window.

I mixed in a few more messages. An Anglo-Indian chair injects a little exoticism, as well as tradition, and a wicker bench introduces another handcrafted element. Despite the complexity due to the contrasts—horizontal and vertical, contemporary and traditional, industrial and handcrafted, solid and void—it's a very clean composition that floats on painted white floors.

Surprise yourself. Is a singer thinking about the next note? Not if she's any good. If you're worried about what comes next, you can't be completely in the emotions of the song. It's the same thing for an actor on stage. If he's trying to remember the next line, he can't be in the moment. Each word has to sound like he just thought it for the first time. The same principle applies to interior decorating.

BENJAMIN MOORE
MUSTANG
2111-30

BENJAMIN MOORE
CORN YELLOW
2161-40

BENJAMIN MOORE
TAOS TAUPE
2111-40

BENJAMIN MOORE
DESERT TAN
2153-50

BENJAMIN MOORE
BARREN PLAIN
2111-60

THERE WASN'T MUCH DESIGN WIGGLE ROOM IN THIS house by Norman Jaffe, a legendary Long Island architect of the 1960s and 1970s. The peaks and angles, wood ceilings, and plank walls all bear his indelible fingerprints. My client loved the house and wanted to remain faithful to the vision. He was adamant that I not alter anything besides the floors. How do you take the house out of its time warp and introduce a new point of view without violating its integrity?

I felt the best approach was to throw in a mixture of elements to loosen the collar a bit. I started by painting the walls white and staining the floors dark to balance the wood ceiling and stone fireplace wall. I brought in a mixture of furnishings from other periods to warm the space and give it a different perspective, while still maintaining Jaffe's architectural approach. An Edwardian chair brings a sense of comfort. Wicker chairs stained the same color as the floors add a casual quality, and Chinese chairs import a different

culture and sensibility. I used some midcentury pieces and a French chaise—a piece of outdoor furniture made of oak—to reinforce the sense of strong architectural lines. A high-backed sofa gives the lofty room a sense of intimacy. To finish it off, a big area rug made of squares of cowhide establishes an island that pulls all of the furniture together. Upholstery fabrics and leather in natural beiges, browns, and taupes meld with the rug, the wood floor, and the stone wall. I tried to blend the house and furnishings so that the interiors looked as though they had been there as long as the house. I didn't want the inside to feel like some new, foreign element. I aspired to a worn and mellow look that would soften the harder edges of the house.

BENJAMIN MOORE
MARS RED
2172-20

BENJAMIN MOORE
NAVAJO RED
2171-10

BENJAMIN MOORE
WROUGHT IRON
2124-10

BENJAMIN MOORE
TROUT GRAY
2124-20

MANY PEOPLE ARE WOWED BY HIGH CEILINGS. BUT from a designer's point of view, they are a mixed blessing because you also want a sense of intimacy. Frank Lloyd Wright said a ceiling higher than eight feet dehumanizes a space.

In the case of this men's library at Liberty National Golf Club, the ceilings were about sixteen feet high, a measurement that will dwarf all the furniture in a room. My approach was to use the rust-colored wool bouclé of the sofa to upholster the back wall in grids. That unifies the wall and the sofa and very subtly brings the space down and anchors it to the floor. The sofa is paired with swivel tub chairs and an ottoman that measures a hefty eight by four feet. Working in a range of tonalities, I upholstered the tub chairs in a brownish velvet and used an aged leather on the ottoman, which helped give the room a cozy quality.

To break up the palette, I covered the pillows in a straw-colored chintz. The yellow brings out the rust. You have to see one color in relation to another to appreciate each. The contrast can be as graphic as black on white or as subtle as brown against rust. But it's important, because contrast helps to define the elements in a space. I also found that in a very tall room like this, a small drop of yellow helped attract the eye and bring it down.

Over the sofa I hung a photograph of the back of a seventeenth-century bronze Thai mirror— a mirror that in reality is only seven inches in diameter but is here blown up to six feet square. You have the impression you're looking at a planet. The corrosion on the bronze gives the photograph the look of a moonscape. Centered in the space, it provides a compelling focal point.

CONNECT

PAPUA NEW GUINEA

The places I pick for my yearly trips are off the beaten path. I want to get away from my day-to-day life and step into another rhythm, connect with a different culture. Recently, I've been exploring the islands of the Indonesian archipelago. I have meandered down the rivers of Borneo on a houseboat and roamed around Irian Jaya, in the western, Indonesian half of New Guinea. When I heard that the eastern half, Papua New Guinea, was even more primitive, with tribes that were still living in complete isolation, I couldn't resist.

For one of the least traveled countries in the world, Papua New Guinea offers a string of mosts: it's the world's highest island and the world's second largest island, and it has the largest area of intact rainforest outside the Amazon. Papuans speak some 850 languages and dialects. But beyond the statistics, it's a plunge into the depths of millennial time, with entire villages and areas living in what anthropologists call "pre-contact"—in cultures as they were before boats and airplanes landed. Or almost. The Papuans still pierce their ears for body jewelry and they still dress for tribal war, but now they freely mix bottle caps and plastics with seashells and feathers in their colorful costumes. Whatever works. You're stepping into a *National Geographic* article.

The capital, Port Moresby, is as provincial and humdrum as a city can get. I visited the National Museum to get an overview of the arts and crafts of the country, something that always fascinates me. I'm interested in purchasing artifacts to send back to my shop, and a mini-education is helpful. Then I went to bed early in order to be ready for my trip to Tari, home of the colorful and very photogenic Huli wigmen.

The airport in Port Moresby is your typical third-world mayhem—a few pale tourists in a sea of Papuan natives, all trying to get to the front of the line. People are pushing, children are screaming, and everyone is laden with luggage—suitcases, mattresses, fruits, vegetables, as well as a few surfboards attached to Australian dudes. There are no railroads, or even many roads, to speak of, and the infrastructure of air travel ties this very mountainous island together. The airplane has left, as it were, a very light footprint on the landscape, which remains quite intact as a result.

The plane was packed. People were chattering—a high-pitched, staccato sound that could have been confused with birds. And then I realized that this is a language that came out of the forest and still has the essence of that place. The landscape out the window looked like a carpet made up of many gradations of green. Rivers snaked through the thick foliage, made even more lush by the rainy season. After two hours in the air, we were informed that due to fog we had to return to Port Moresby and try again another day. But the next flight wasn't until three days later! I quickly

decided to rearrange my itinerary, booking a flight to Rabaul. Rabaul is the capital of New Britain, the largest of the offshore islands.

After three hours of stops and layovers, my feet finally touched land, and it felt like paradise—fields of coconut trees covered with blooming orchid plants, a soft breeze, and a sense of tranquility and the easy life. It was a twenty-minute drive to the Rapopo Plantation Resort, where my room was in a timbered pavilion right on the ocean. I immediately went for a swim, and the water was just as I like it—hot-tub temperature. All those hours in airports and on crowded planes melted away. At night, when I walked back to my room after dinner—very good lobster—the lawn was dotted with frogs happily croaking away.

In the morning, I drove out to see the original Rabaul, which was buried under six feet of ash in 1994 when two of the local volcanoes erupted simultaneously. Luckily, very few people were hurt. Most of the town is still abandoned and eerie, entombed in ash. You can see the remains of buildings. The whole island is little more than a chain of volcanoes, and one or the other is usually smoking. The sand on the beaches is black. At one beach, the water is bubbling hot and the locals often come here to cook their food.

To travel New Britain is a flashback to World War II. The remains of Japanese planes and tanks are scattered all over, some under water, where they have become an attraction for scuba divers. You can also peer into the caves and bunkers where Japanese soldiers lived after invading the island in 1941. The Japanese also left their genetic imprint: many natives have Asian features that are the result of the Japanese occupation.

More interesting to me than the Japanese artifacts of war was the Baining tribe, a people who adhere to their own very distinct customs up in the mountains. They are known for their fire dance. It takes weeks to prepare the ritual. First, the men of the tribe pound bark until it's almost like paper and make masks in the shapes of different animals, birds, and butterflies. They're painted with eyes and festooned with feathers. Each represents a different spirit. The women are not allowed to see the masks until the ceremony, which was scheduled to take place the night I arrived. Of course I had to see it. I was happy, and lucky, to have rearranged my trip.

A bonfire is lit in the middle of a clearing, and after dark, when most of the flames have subsided into red-hot embers, the fire dancers appear wearing their masks. Possessed by the different spirits, they dance around the fire and in and over the embers. Two of the men hold snakes about three feet long, which they lift into the air as they walk over the hot coals. Around and around they dance, jumping over the flames in an almost hypnotic state, embracing the spirits of the jungle. It's pitch dark, no light except that from the fire, which picks out the faces of the women and children who are watching and making barking and chattering noises. Other men pound wood logs that have been hollowed out and beat drums. It's a rhythmic, throbbing sound that gradually builds to a climax. I didn't really want to make eye contact with those snakes, or the men holding them, because I was petrified that they were going to bring them over to me.

Snakes happen to be one of my phobias. There was a time when even a photo of a snake would freak me out. You can put a toad in my hand, I have eaten live bugs, but a snake is just . . . There's something about that forked tongue and those slitlike eyes. As I was standing there watching the dance, I was exhilarated. But there was also a frisson of danger. Are they going to come over and put the snake on me? Then, suddenly, the dance seemed to be over, and the men were heading into the forest. My guide motioned me to follow. Really? Am I about to be the human sacrifice? It turned out that the men were headed to another clearing, and another fire, away from the women, where they took off their masks and burned them. Two men raised machetes and swiftly chopped up the snakes; the rest of the men reached over, picked up the pieces, and ate them raw. The snakes gather great power over the course of the ritual, and now the men possessed that power. I was getting nervous again. What should I do if they offered me some? Smile and refuse, or would that be offensive? But I was not put to the test. The ceremony was over and we left.

The next morning I was on a plane to Wewak for the next phase of my journey—a canoe trip down the Sepik River. Once we landed, I met my guide and got into a truck loaded with provisions, including maximum-strength sunscreen and mosquito repellant. Because of the rainy season, mosquitoes were every-

where. You could look down and see twenty of them on your arms and legs, in sizes ranging from small to medium to huge. Malaria is a risk. I kept drenching myself in mosquito repellant. After a bumpy, four-hour ride, we arrived in Pagwi. There was the canoe, hollowed out of a tree trunk about fifty feet long and equipped with a Yamaha motor and a crew of three.

Once we were on the river, the cool breeze helped alleviate the intense heat. I was just getting comfortable, relaxing into slow, languorous river mode, when suddenly there was some excitement on the boat. The motormen pointed out a wild pig crossing the river. We headed toward it to give me a better chance at a photograph—or so I thought. As soon as we got near, they started to hit it over the head with the paddle. Before I knew what was going on, one of the guys jumped in and grabbed the pig while the others kept hitting it. Then another guy jumped in, and the two drowned the pig. With great pride and joy, they raised their thumbs in victory, shouting, "With stick we killed the pig!" I felt like I was in the midst of *Lord of the Flies.* We pulled to the side of the river where there was a hut, and within minutes the motormen had

gutted and cut up the pig, splitting it with the man of the hut. They told me that it was a good omen. The river was welcoming me, and we would have this animal for dinner. When we reached our accommodations for the night—two huts—they roasted the wild pig in a pit for three hours and then cooked it with coconut milk and chili. It was a feast for all of us.

In the morning, we got up at 5:30 to get back in the canoe. I don't know why, in this context, I was still looking at my watch. Time on the Sepik is different from time on the clock at Grand Central. We paddled along in the canoe for a ways and then pulled over and hiked into the forest to get to an area where the birds of paradise congregate. This was my chance to see their mating dance. They fly from one tree to the next, flapping their light brown wings and shaking the yellowish-white feathers on their tails. We spent the rest of the day crossing Chambri Lake and exploring small tributaries of the river. The forest canopies on each bank almost met over our heads. Flying between the trees were egrets, parrots, hawks, and eagles. I saw magnificent butterflies eight inches wide, in extraordinary colors. I kept looking for snakes coiling around

trees, but never saw any. As we were going down one small river, I heard what sounded like a sawmill. My immediate reaction was, Oh no, civilization has arrived. I was shocked to find out that the source of the noise was a small insect, not more than one inch long. That was the sound it made with its wings.

The next morning brought the first full day of rain, which started in the middle of the night. There is nothing so nice as lying in bed reading while torrential rains come down. I kept thinking of Gloria Swanson as Sadie Thompson. In the afternoon, we got back in the canoe and floated through a sea of water hyacinth on our way to Palembei village. The people of this region are known for their intricate carvings representing crocodiles and various spirits, all painted and inlaid with cowry shells. They are displayed in a spirit house, which is the heart of the cultural life of the village. It's a large rectangular building on stilts, which protect it from the periodic floods; I was told to think of it as a church. It is where initiation ceremonies take place. When a boy reaches the age of twenty, his back and arms are cut in a traditional crocodile design to create the scars that prove his manhood.

The crocodile is deeply embedded in the Palembei mythology. In the village of Yentchen, I had a ring-side seat for the *singsing*, a ritual crocodile dance. The men dress in the spirit house and come out bearing a crocodile about eight feet long woven from bamboo and decorated with cowry-shell eyes and wood teeth and scales. The women and children follow a warrior, dressed in a leaf skirt with a painted body, who carries a spear to kill the crocodile. Meanwhile the crocodile opens and closes his mouth, taunting the women and children, as they all dance to the beat of drums and circle the spirit house three times.

The next night I went on my own crocodile hunt. Our prey would provide skins for the villagers to sell, as well as dinner. We started out in two canoes and met three more as we headed down the river. It was 8:00 and very dark. We paddled slowly, almost glid-ing, while the men in the prow of the boat shined a strong flashlight on the water. I was told that it was not a good idea to go after too big a crocodile, say eight or ten feet long, because it could swing around and topple the boat with its tail—in which case dinner would be a different course.

In the sweep of the light, the surface of the water was dotted with what looked like pairs of small red light bulbs. The hunters can tell the size of the crocodile by the distance between the eyes. They plunge their spear, which consists of a long stick with multiple spikes at the end, into the tail of the crocodile and pull him into the boat with lightning speed, accompanied by much shouting and screaming. The mouth of the crocodile is quickly tied shut, its legs are roped together, and it becomes remarkably passive. The first one we caught was four feet long, the second five feet, and the last four feet. I was told that the hides of saltwater crocodiles, which are yellow and black, are more valuable than those of freshwater crocodiles, which are white and black. The other canoes caught similar numbers, and we headed back to the village. There the crocodiles were killed and skinned and the meat divided among the families who had participated. I tried not to judge. These people have been hunting for hundreds of years, and their respect for nature is very evolved, much more than ours. Hunting is for food, not pleasure. When we got back to our house, the meat was cooked and wrapped in banana leaves with greens, chili, onions, and lime juice. It was served with rice, cooked in coconut milk, and it was delicious.

On the return journey, it rained all the way to Pagwi, where I got back into the truck to Wewak for the flight to Port Moresby. I was looking forward to the last leg of my trip, to Tari. Once thought to be uninhabited, the Tari Basin was discovered by gold prospectors in 1930 and then found to have a population of close to one million. From the moment you land, it's a trip into another era. First, there is no airport, just a landing field, a fence, and a gate with a crowd of people. Some are here just to see the small planes that land twice a week.

Unlike the tribes along the Sepik, famous for carving wood objects ranging from utensils to their magnificent spirit houses, the Huli wigmen use their own bodies as artistic canvases. Fully decked out with body decoration, face painting, and human-hair wigs, and dressed to the nines in elaborate, highly colored, all-organic outfits, the men are stunning. Like male birds of paradise, they wear the plumage; the females are less colorful, more workaday. Women strap classic string bilum bags on their heads to help carry large loads. They wear black to their weddings.

But the men are not just narcissists all set for the runway. These are warriors preparing for battle, or at least *singsings*, and they draw their inspiration from the Tari Basin's fertile and swampy valleys, which are ringed by rugged mountains teeming with birds. Nature for the Huli is one big aviary, and the Huli dress to match. Men venerate the many varieties of birds of paradise in everyday and ceremonial life by decorating their human-hair wigs with feathers taken from the most beautiful specimens. The warriors also weave daisies and cuscus (possum) fur into their wigs and paint their faces with yellow and red ochre. Outdoing themselves in what must be a fiercely competitive fashion arena, the warriors pierce their nasal septa with cassowary quills and top out their body art by carrying surreal, multicolored umbrellas. Even the birds of paradise have cause, and pause, for jealousy.

The Huli have this time to devote to themselves because they don't have television, and because they live in a version of paradise, residing in homesteads scattered across beautiful, carefully cultivated valleys. In this fertile soil some ten thousand years ago, they may have been the first people to start controlled agriculture.

From the viewpoint of consumer society, these people are not only nearly pre-contact but also pre-Walmart. They feed themselves and dress themselves by themselves. They barter. Traditionally, they wear their currency in the form of jewelry, particularly precious shells from the distant sea. These are people who admire nature, from within the nature they are part of. There is zero degree of separation.

CONNECT

STILL LIFES

IN TODAY'S MARKETPLACE, it's possible to get great objects through catalogs. Wisteria has reproductions with a nice patina, and West Elm and Restoration Hardware each have a strong design sensibility and point of view. I'm spoiled because of VW Home, my own source of objects right across the hall from my office. I'm able to buy things that are out of the ordinary and suit my quirky sensibility, things that bring a sense of crustiness and character to a job.

This cabinet, from the Martha Stewart catalog, is the basis for a play on still lifes. I hung a framed poster of watering cans and a pear low to the cabinet top. The watering cans seem to commingle with some old pitchers, as though the watering cans freely step in and out of the frame in a three-dimensional still life. The ears of corn I threw in a bowl pick up the pear, again three-dimensionalizing the two-dimensional. Nothing here is expensive, or even inviolable. Add more pitchers, more fruit, move them around, enjoy composing. It's all loose, fungible, inviting.

Being a good designer means plugging into the wavelength of the person who hired you. I want to connect a room to your experiences so that it represents you, your passions, and your point of view.

THE FIRST THING YOU SEE in a house is the entrance foyer, and you want it to give a good first impression, like a strong handshake. It should also give a glimpse of what style or mood lies ahead. But the fore-shadowing needn't be elaborate. It can be as simple as introducing a color that will reappear later. And you should create a focal point to catch the eye. I'll often do a grouping of objects on a tabletop. The goal is to come up with a composition of elements that have a sense of romance or surprise.

If you're creating a tablescape, it's important to look at the table itself. The objects can go with it, sharing the same style, or they can set up an opposite effect. Here I thought it would be interesting to combine a Dutch table, with all its curves and bulbous shapes, with urns that I had made in India. (Actually, they're hookah pipes in marble. I started with the classic shape and then blew up the scale, keeping the proportions.) I like the way the urns nearly mimic the shapes of the legs. The curves play against the straight lines of the steel panels on the wall. Everything here is vertical—the tall stems of the orchid, the stalk of bamboo in a photograph I took, although the bamboo leaves do slash across the stalk on a dramatic diagonal. Most people would not pick up on the verticality, but it's a subliminal visual message that subtly pulls the whole setting together. That the knuckles of the bamboo have been enlarged adds a note of visual surprise. You remember the irrational more than things that are perfectly polite.

BENJAMIN MOORE
TANGY ORANGE
2014-30

I OFTEN DO THINGS IN THREES. The number has great significance spiritually and numerologically, but that's not the reason I do it. To me, three just feels right. It doesn't have to be three of the same thing. It can just be three objects that complement each other.

In this window niche in the stairway of a Nantucket house, I stacked and staggered three lacquered orange cubes. Then I arranged three mounted bronze Thai trays, six hundred years old, on and around the cubes. The vertical complements the horizontal, and the circle, the square, like yin and yang. Your eye focuses on the trays as you come up the staircase. The tight, angular geometry frames the setting beautifully, and the white walls silhouette the vibrant cubes and dark bronzes. A single flower brings a sense of something alive to the display.

BENJAMIN MOORE
PALE DAFFODIL
2017-60

SOMETIMES MY COMPOSITIONS are very simple, composed of just a couple of elements. Here a thin floating shelf, supported by brackets recessed into a wall, holds a pair of Burmese spinning tops, which look very sculptural against a sprig of yellow and a Cindy Sherman photograph. A shelf like this works well where space is tight and you don't have enough room for a piece of furniture.

In another entryway, a shelf holds a photograph of Papuan mudmen taken by Irving Penn, a tray of paperwhites, and a pair of Italian lights looking a bit like abstract penguins. The setting is activated by natural light coming through a slot in a side wall, which washes the textured concrete surfaces and strikes the photograph and flowers. Light can make a still life come alive. It sculpts objects.

With the right lighting, you can create a high-impact focal point without spending much money. A cone of light can single out a flower on a shelf, and that may be all the room needs. A lot of drama comes from light alone. Many times I use a Parentesi lamp, which is an adjustable spot that glides up and down a taut wire. I also use recessed miniature PAR lights, which can be aimed at a particular object, making almost anything look like a piece of sculpture.

Always think about the background as part of the setting. By creating a texture on the wall behind the shelf, whether it's rough concrete, stainless steel, upholstered panels, or just plain color, you add another layer to the composition, a backdrop that begins to work as a visual binder to whatever you're putting on the shelf. Uplights give you another alternative with the potential for a lot of drama, especially if you're working with a free-standing piece of furniture you can pull away from a wall, allowing the light to bathe the wall from below.

A DEAD SPACE AT THE ENTRANCE to this bedroom was the perfect place for a free-standing table that could lead into the room. I chose a strong, almost cubic Chinese table that became the podium for a cross-cultural still life. The lantern came from Paris, the bas-relief patinated copper bowl from India, and the mother-of-pearl tray from Thailand. The pieces all relate by their age and authenticity; curiously they triangulate through history as artifacts of three great cultures. I love to use candles in foyers, and here a candle in the lantern lets my client change the mood with the strike of a match.

HERE I'VE MADE A DOUBLE COMPOSITION: first, a table-scape on a tray, and second, the tray on a tufted ottoman framed by a mantel sculpted in stone. The size escalates from the diminutive scale of the smallest object to the sub-architectural scale of the mantel.

Tibetan neckpieces made out of coral and turquoise bring very precise dots of color to this neutral setting. I added two wooden boxes I bought in Syria, inlaid in silver. I bought the 1940s mantel in France, and I like it because it's transitional, both classical and abstract. As a background, it's clean and unfussy. Black slate fills the space between the two vertical supports. A potted orchid on the tray springs into the space of the mantel, diplomatically bridging the scale of the two compositions.

BENJAMIN MOORE
CEMENT GRAY
2112-60

BENJAMIN MOORE
FLAME
2012-20

TO HIDE OR NOT TO HIDE THE TV? That is the question. I always say to clients, do you want to put a doily over your telephone? That's the same, to me, as trying to hide the TV. It's a major component of our lives, so make a place for it. If the setting is thought out, it can become an asset to the space. In this room, the TV is set on a long, low cabinet that also holds books. The open shelf makes it feel less massive, and the drawers can store DVDs.

The upholstered screen behind it has an interesting effect. It adds another layer and another texture to the space. The folds play with the light, which focuses your eye on the total setting. Balanced by the topiaries and the bronze hand, the TV becomes just one part of a fuller composition.

EVEN IF A PIECE OF FURNITURE IS UTILITARIAN, like a bench or a card table or a media unit, it can form part of a wonderful setting. This lovely antique Filipino piece is little more than a cupboard, but the unfussy lines and overall shape bring out the natural grains of the wood. The simplicity begged for more simplicity, so I gathered a little collection of Indian milk containers, also made of wood, atop the cabinet. I placed the cabinet at a jog in the wall and then set it all off with a minimal curtain to create a niche.

The rudimentary simplicity of this rural grouping contrasts with the modernist sophistication of the room beyond. I'm mixing messages. The cabinet makes a big impact beyond the niche because of the power of significant detail and the sheer gravity of authenticity.

BENJAMIN MOORE
JADE GARDEN
2056-20

BENJAMIN MOORE
BABY CHICK
2023-20

I'VE BEEN USING LARGE-SCALE OTTOMANS since 1991, when I first designed one in a collection for Henredon. The appeal it had for people was that they could put their feet up and still have a coffee table. The simple idea of a double-use, hybrid piece of furniture is still going strong after twenty-five years.

The trays were a natural progression from the ottoman. People needed a surface on which to put down drinks; as a designer, what I got out of the juxtaposition was the contrast between the hardness of the tray and the softness of the ottoman. In this room, the Murano glass sculpture on the tray and the bunch of wildflowers add a splash of yellow.

The subtext of arrangements like this is that the ottoman relaxes the space, even if it's elegant and even if it's practical. The usefulness comes in with the addition of the large-scale trays. I've done them as big as thirty by thirty-six inches, and the ottomans can go up to seven feet long by three feet wide. Some of my clients joke that extra guests can sleep on the coffee table.

A client will come into my office and say, this chair is great. I'll ask, what is it that you like? Is it the color? The shape? Or the softness of the upholstery?

A BENCH IS A VERSATILE PIECE OF FURNITURE. It can be pulled over to a seating group or a dining table to provide an extra seat. But when it's not being used as a chair, it becomes a decorative element, another surface on which to arrange things.

I took a lantern from Pottery Barn, a bowl of fruit, and a vase of flowers and set them down on this Chinese bench. Casual and uncontrived, it's a little vignette by the window that catches your eye. A painting is just propped on the windowsill. One of the secrets to making a room feel alive is for things to look as though they could move and change at any minute instead of being tethered to one spot forever.

BENJAMIN MOORE
ANTIQUE PEARL
2113-70

A side table is another opportunity. Start with the shape of the table itself. There are no rules that say it has to be a plain rectangle. The curves and the interesting legs of this wrought-iron table bring softness and character to the space. I like to find at least one unexpected thing to put on top, like these three swordfish swords. They came from Thailand, the window screens on the wall came from China, and the fabric covering the pillow is African kuba cloth. I covered the walls of the room in grasscloth to add another layer of texture.

I SPEND A LOT OF TIME CONSIDERING the best way to display artwork. Once you nail something to the wall, you stop seeing it after a few months. And if you remove it, you need to repaint the walls. My solution is picture ledges. You can alter the arrangement anytime you want, according to your mood. Adding a new piece doesn't require a total rethinking of the walls. And objects can be displayed alongside the artwork, which makes for interesting juxtapositions.

Now that picture ledges are sold by retailers, you no longer have to make them yourself. (Although it's not that hard—you just buy a molding from the hardware store and cut it to fit.) I like picture ledges in hallways and children's rooms. They can turn any wall into a focal point. I usually place them at fifty-four inches from the floor. I've found that's a good height for viewing as you walk by, but of course it depends on the size of the artwork. If you have the ceiling height, do more than one ledge.

There was no room for anything interesting, like a piece of antique furniture, in this tight bedroom. But a picture ledge brings a sense of depth to the space and makes a narrow room feel wider. It's an opportunity to play with objects while still keeping the rest of the surfaces clean, and it brings a modern sensibility to the space.

WHEN YOU'RE CREATING A TABLESCAPE, you have to read the objects and find a cohesive balance between them. Here is a collection of birds' eggs, an old clock face, and ivory and tortoiseshell boxes. The coloration is all very neutral, and then I added a vase full of flowers.

Why does it work? The objects on the right are close together. The items overlap. The heights vary from small to medium to large. And everything is tied together by that subdued palette. Then the flowers on the left balance it out. The color and the shape create an equivalent mass. It's different, but it all feels right together.

I love compositions within compositions, like an assortment of seashells in a shadow box. They create their own pattern, and then I play off it with more shapes—a finial from a building and a tall, thin topiary. I'm mixing textures and heights and shapes, natural and man-made, but it works. The array entices the eye.

BOOKS ARE ONE OF THE STRONGEST elements you can bring into a room (especially if you read them). For the most part, I use bookcases for books, without inserting a lot of accessories. Still, bookends or objects that become a pattern within a bookcase appeal to me. Entire walls and rooms can become settings.

In this dining room, I picked up an idea from the apartment Billy Baldwin did for Cole Porter. He used bookcases to line and define the rooms. Here, one shelf holds liquor and soda and glasses, so the space doubles as a bar and a library. With a piano, the room becomes a complete entertaining environment.

Most of my clients are shocked when I remove paper covers from books. I find books look so much richer when all you see are the bindings. Then you get subtle variations in color. I do, however, leave covers on picture books. A small detail like removing the covers, repeated across scores of books, can have a strong impact on a space.

———————

They say that in order to move forward, you need to bring the past with you. That may be one of the reasons I like antiques. They connect us to where we all came from, in a global sense. They carry our history. A piece doesn't have to be five hundred years old to be valuable to me. It doesn't matter whether it's a Louis XVI chair or a crude African stool. I just want something that speaks of another culture or another time.

BENJAMIN MOORE
ICING ON THE
CAKE
2049-70

BENJAMIN MOORE
SLATE BLUE
1648

BENJAMIN MOORE
MOZART BLUE
1665

NOTICE ANYTHING UNUSUAL about this eighteenth-century English mirror? Instead of hanging on the wall, it's floating in thin air. The art of this particular composition is in the unusual method of display. The mirror is suspended from the ceiling on very strong fishing wire, which is practically invisible. With no evident means of support, the vignette as a whole takes on a surreal quality. The bedside table, with its front faced in mirror, also almost dematerializes. Its rectilinear lines balance the curlicues on the mirror, and the curtain provides a soft backdrop. It could have been a throwaway moment—after all, how many things can you do with a bedside table? But now that mirror floating in space is what everyone remembers of the room.

BANGKOK MARKET

I'M OFTEN ASKED WHERE I FIND the objects for my still life compositions. When I travel, I'm a vacuum cleaner, hoovering up the finds I come across, often serendipitously. I buy only things that I love, even if I have no immediate use for them or no client in mind. I'm acquisitive without being possessive. I don't hoard my finds in my own loft but park them in my showroom, VW Home, which is open to both the public and designers. It's a resource that fills a void, at least in New York, for objects that have a feeling of authenticity about them. It's not commercial, not from a mall. I draw on the changing collection when a particular project and a particular client call for pieces. Sometimes it pains me to part with a unique item, but mostly I'm happy to see it settle into a suitable home, whether on a table or in a grouping, as though part of a still life.

I'm on safari on all of my trips, hunting down objects in flea markets and souks and antiques fairs around the world. But there's nothing quite like the Sunday market in Bangkok for range and depth and

exoticism, not to mention rawness of experience. It's a microcosm of the culture, almost a snapshot of the Thai collective unconscious. You learn a lot about a country when individuals sell wares directly to the public, without the varnish of a formal store or corporation. It's also pure pleasure to stroll in the cacophony of a million things vying for your attention.

The market sets up on Friday and stays open until Sunday. You can buy dogs, T-shirts, underwear, perfume, antiques, orchids, light bulbs, lamps, water lilies, ceramics, silk flowers, artworks, butterflies, fabrics, sheets, bathrobes, incense—you name it. When I go to Bangkok, I aim to be there for at least three weekend markets. It took me a good three years before I could find my way through the rows and

spend at least ten minutes walking up and down the alleys to find him. And even with something in mind, it's a little frustrating, like being let loose in a candy shop without anything to put candy in. You don't know what to grab first, and you can't take it all. The market has changed over the years, and now you see pickers selling to bigger shops and antiques dealers buying on their own.

I suppose I'm one of the dealers because I'm buying for the shop. In the furniture section, I buy Burmese furniture, cabinets, monk's benches, drums, teak paneling salvaged from old houses, seventeenth-century pottery, bronze mirrors, bronze bowls, lacquerware, mother-of-pearl trays, bracelets made out of jade, textiles, and fragments of Buddhas and temples. Over the years I've learned that what you find one year you may never see again. I don't know in advance how I'm going to use the pieces, but I believe that objects of a high quality always work with each other, even across periods and styles. Quality is what will bind objects on a tabletop or in a room.

rows of little stalls, with thousands and thousands of people. On Sundays, it's like rush hour on the subway. It's seven times the size of Clignancourt, the big Paris flea market. Humongous. You have to get there early, and you should know where you want to go and how much you want to pay. I find the best place to start is in the area that sells furniture, pottery objects, and bronzes.

When I first started attending, it was a bit over-whelming, with people behaving like locusts, pushing and shoving. If you don't know where you're going, you think you'll never find the same place twice. One man who has a stall with old bells is slightly out of the way; though I have bought from him over the years, I

I'm buying, I'm paying, I'm photographing and measuring each item I acquire. I write every purchase down in a book. I go to the bank and get cash bundled with rubber bands and figure out who gets what.

THAT'S HOW I FIND OBJECTS AND ACCESSORIES, but it could be the flea markets in Manhattan, though they're vanishing, or the Brimfield Antique Show and Flea Market, which is still thriving, or L'Isle-sur-la-Sorgue in the south of France, a great alternative to Clignancourt in Paris, which has been picked over. But I travel off the beaten track, and markets like the one in Bangkok make sense in my life. Everyone has his or her own patterns, and the hunt should reinforce what seems natural.

Then I take my discoveries to a man who creates the stands on which they'll be mounted. It's a day-long process, after which I go back to the Oriental, one of my favorite hotels anywhere, and lie by the pool for a couple of hours to recover. Even there, I'm reviewing the photos, relishing the intricacy of the carvings, admiring the refinement of the lacquerwork and paintings. It's the satisfaction after the hunt.

Back in the studio, when I'm working on a project, there comes a moment for a finishing touch. It's like when the painter selects the frame for his painting or the chef throws in a dash of cilantro to spike the flavor of a soup. For me, it's often a smaller object or objects. I think of them as the building blocks of the more intimate part of a design, the features that your eye looks for and settles on, the things that pique your curiosity. These are the details that make the room and complete a thought.

AS I LOOK AT THE PLAN, I think of the space as I enter it: how will I live there? If I'm going to sit on a sofa, I'll probably focus on the coffee table. If I'm getting into bed at night, I'll glance at a night table. Those are the moments when you pivot off wonderful objects that complement each other in a setting. A TV might even be part of the overall picture. Just where is your eye going to land? Where does the space need a punch or a shot of color? You're putting in something round because everything else in a setting is square. You're looking for something old, something crude, because the room is leaning midcentury modern. A room with dominant horizontal lines might need something vertical.

Which objects would balance out a space? How would you make a composition? Mixing pieces from different times and origins is not simply a matter of cleverly juxtaposing styles. It's cross-cultural. In a grouping, each element comments on the other. The conversation is not just visual.

CONNECT
ENVIRONMENTS

I know how to paddle a canoe. But I approach each river in a different way. Each time a working relationship begins, I start from square one. It's often difficult for people to articulate what they want. So I have to discover it for myself, by asking questions. That's why I've developed a questionnaire, which I ask every client to fill out. If you start to design a project without having all the information you need, it's like starting a trip without a map. I need to know where I'm starting from in order to get to where I'm going.

———————

AN OPEN DOORWAY IN A CRISP WALL OF SHARPLY CUT stone introduces the "Alice moment" at this house in Malibu. You park your car on one side of the massive wall and then you step through the opening, emerging in a different world. You've left land behind for garden, sea, and sky.

The elegantly cut gateway is part of a long stone wall that eventually becomes the side of the house, and the run of wall hides the view as you approach. On the other side, glass takes over from stone: transparent glass railings leave the view unobstructed as it stretches out to sea. Steps lead up several levels to the front door.

That simple wall with the cut-out door not only frames the view but also establishes nature—earth, sea, air, sky, ocean, greenery—as the subject of the house. The stone relates to the land through the craftsmanship of natural materials. The design is all about living the California dream, in a house that's at one with nature.

MOST CHILDREN WHO SPLIT THEIR TIME BETWEEN parents living separately have to adjust to the environment of each parent. But in this case, my client wanted to create a child-friendly home where his kids and their friends could hang out and not feel a sense of formality or strictness. The boys could play video games, listen to music, and watch movies. It would also be a space where the father could entertain his friends. Dads need to hang out, too.

I removed the walls between the living and dining rooms to connect them and open up the space. The existing dining room has been converted into what we used to call a den; today we might call it a hangout place. Now when you enter the apartment, you walk straight toward a baby grand piano. Baby grands, with that curve, always add grace to a space. Then you can pivot toward the living room on the left or the den on the right. The piano makes the space feel open but not empty and, in combination with a painting, creates a great focal point.

The return on an L-shaped sofa separates the foyer, den, and living room without obstructing the view. The space looks like one large open area, but without feeling like an empty field. The colors flow from left to right. On the living room side, I mainly used blue with touches of rust, and on the den side, I did rust with touches of blue.

I try to connect my creative vision to the client's reality. I need to understand not just the elements of a space but how my client is going to use it. What are their likes and dislikes? What will make them comfortable? You sort of put on their clothing as you start working out the design.

BENJAMIN MOORE
WATERTOWN
818

BENJAMIN MOORE
GOLD RUSH
2166-10

BENJAMIN MOORE
IMPERIAL
YELLOW
314

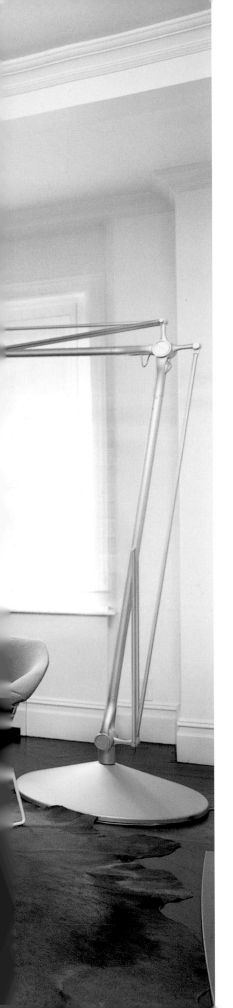

In the most successful rooms, the
personality of the client comes through.
If a client is very formal, the space will
be more traditional and precise.
If they're more loose and casual, the
space will feel equally laid back.

I didn't want to see a sofa in the living room
and another one in the den, so in the den I installed
a big framed bed where the boys could all jump in
and be casual. Beanbags on the floor give them one
more area to be just kids. And the circular Harry
Bertoia chair is for the token grown-up. There are
two TVs, to keep peace in the family, one on each
side of the divide between living room and den.
Adults can watch in the living room while the kids
crash in the den, and vice versa. All the materials we
used—leathers, cowhide, bouclé—are child-friendly
and durable.

Flat-screen TVs provide an opportunity to
create different display strategies. In Paris I found a
company that has made artists' easels since the turn
of the last century, and I've been using these pieces
with great success for mounting televisions. The
easels give you the flexibility to move the screen up
and down. Tubular cables hide all the wires and
create a clean installation.

MANY YEARS AGO, WHILE TRAVELING IN SWEDEN, I saw an arrangement of six horizontal mirrors stacked in two groups of three. I liked the way the assembly reflected slices of the room and thought it was much more interesting than just a plain mirrored wall. This type of array can transform a dull corner into a fascinating place of its own. In this seating area, a dark tobacco-colored fabric on the banquette picks up the tones of a Tabriz rug on the floor. Then I topped a contemporary table with eighteenth-century Italian candlesticks. I love their baroque curves and the gleam of the gilt— it's like a piece of jewelry for the room.

I'VE DESIGNED MANY DIFFERENT KINDS OF KITCHEN islands: contemporary islands, old-fashioned islands. I've even found antique tables and turned them into islands. I like an island to look like a piece of furniture, rather than a built-in. And I like big islands. I think they offer much-needed workspace as well as a central focus. But rarely have I done an island quite this big—sixteen feet long by nine feet wide. The large size presents a whole new challenge. How do you keep it from looking like a ship has landed smack in the middle of the kitchen?

First, I designed a banquette for one end, which masks the size, and set a breakfast table in front of it. One side of the island is devoted to storage cabinets. On the other side, there's a niche underneath with stools, so the kids can sit there and do their homework. We installed a prep sink on the end near the stove, to concentrate the work area at one end and leave the rest of the space open for other activities.

In a kitchen this size, you want a variety of materials so the room does not become monotonous. The upper cabinets are framed in zinc or teak, with frosted glass doors. The lower cabinets are made of wood or zinc, and the countertops are marble or soapstone. The client wanted the house to have a mixture of old and new, so I tried to bring in a few elements that had a sense of age. The oven hood is made of tarnished copper, and some of the wood has a driftwood finish to make it look as if it had already weathered.

BENJAMIN MOORE
PENNY
2163-30

BENJAMIN MOORE
SAINT MARTIN
SAND
2164-50

BENJAMIN MOORE
STONE WHITE
2120-70

Choosing a designer is like choosing an artist to do your portrait. You want to find an artist whose style fits yours. How do you see yourself? Whose style do you respond to? The more information you can give a designer, the better he can do his job. Like a portrait painter, a designer will do his own interpretation of what he sees in front of him.

———

SO MANY APARTMENTS IN NEW YORK ARE PLAIN OLD boxes, and I'm always trying to throw in a few curves. A large curving sofa gives a sweep to this living room and softens the corner. But what do you do with that gap behind the sofa? My solution here was a paneled screen that adds another dimension to that corner.

At the left end of the sofa, a slab of stainless steel is propped against the wall. It acts as a more contemporary version of a mirror and doubles the light from the windows. A second slab of stainless steel stands opposite it, to the right of a two-toned banquette. It's unusual to do two kinds of upholstery on the same chair, but I wanted to keep playing with the fabrics I had used at the other end of the room. If you pull the two armchairs up, you could serve an intimate dinner to a small group of friends at this table.

WHEN I'M CONFRONTED WITH A SMALL ROOM, I often choose to go dark. Dark tones can be very powerful and take your mind off the size. This bathroom in gunmetal gray has a sense of masculine warmth. A wall-to-wall mirror makes a tight space feel larger.

WHY NOT ADD A LITTLE DRAMA TO A POWDER ROOM? These dark mahogany walls could be straight out of a gentleman's club, but the stainless-steel toilet and sink take it in a different direction. The sink is cantilevered off a floor-to-ceiling mirror. The room has a sense of elegance and drama.

I'M ALWAYS THINKING ABOUT THE VISTAS WITHIN A space. When you look down a hallway, it's not particularly interesting if all you see is a blank wall. You need a focal point. Here, a Sri Lankan cabinet with beautiful lines provides a place for the eye to rest. Instead of hiding the structural supports within the wall, I exposed the industrial I-beams. I like the rough, raw look of the steel columns against the smooth white walls. They seem to come up out of the dark-stained floor like trees.

The various elements in this little passageway become a visual essay on contrasting textures. To make the point even clearer, I added a brick insert to the polished wood floor, under the skylight. The brick gives you a sense of the earth, the handcrafted cabinet gives you a sense of history, and the raw steel columns give you a sense of the contemporary. A pile of logs, stored here for the fireplace, adds more texture. So the space swings from rough to polished, handcrafted to industrial, rustic to contemporary. The mix gives it more depth.

One of the greatest gifts you can have as a designer is the ability to find connections between disparate things. I may put a Sepik wood carving next to a Chinese porcelain vase because I see something similar in the purity of their shapes, or because I like the contrast of the rough and the smooth. I may see a connection between a midcentury modern chair and an Edwardian-style sofa, even though most people wouldn't think they belong in the same room. It's all about finding the objects and the forms and the colors that speak to each other.

_____

Think of bed linens as another accessory, just as important as the pictures on the wall or the objects on the night table. Beautiful sheets and pillowcases bring a sense of luxury to the space. I like to combine different textures on the bed, but not too many colors. Varying shades of the same color are more restful.

BENJAMIN MOORE
SLEIGH BELLS
1480

BENJAMIN MOORE
HERBAL ESCAPE
1487

BENJAMIN MOORE
BLUE HEATHER
1648

BENJAMIN MOORE
STILLWATER
1650

BENJAMIN MOORE
BLUE SPRUCE
1665

I LOVE DESIGNING A BEDROOM. IT'S A ROOM WHERE romance can be blatant, where vulnerability is permitted and intimacy reigns. The bed is the focus, and that's where I start. The design of this bed began with a piece of carved and gilded wood that I found in an antique shop. I worked with my frame maker to extend its dimensions so I could turn it into a headboard. Then I surrounded the antique headboard with a steel canopy frame, connecting old and new, traditional and contemporary. The steel frame creates a room within a room, and that touch of gold on the Rococo curves of the headboard makes the bed feel like a little jewel box.

This bedroom faces the Pacific Ocean and gets a lot of light, and the light is a participant in creating the mood. It plays over the upholstered wall behind the bed and picks out the plush curves. The fabric softens the room and gives it another dimension. I chose silk taffeta for the curtains at the windows because silk has a lovely sheen. Then I lacquered the ceiling to add more shimmer. The textures are sensuous. They give the room a touch of Hollywood glamour.

The real luxury in a bathroom is natural light. But this bathroom had no windows, so I was forced to borrow light from the adjacent bedroom. Here's how I did it. I replaced a solid wall between the two rooms with a wall of frosted glass, which lets in the sun and bathes the bathroom in a soft, even light. I helped the airy effect along by facing the other three walls, and the floor, in white limestone.

The tub is made of pure white marble, and I treated it like a piece of sculpture by letting it stand alone. It feels vaguely Roman, like something you might see in Pompeii. The sinks are also made out of what looks like a block of marble. They feel almost primitive in contrast to the dark, sleek, cantilevered cabinets. The mirrors above them are set on stanchions a few inches in front of the frosted glass. It's a very modern room. When you're inside, you feel as if you're floating in an ethereal limestone-and-glass cube. Then the marble tub and sinks bring in an archaic element. Two different eras are suddenly connected.

If you do a room and buy everything new, it's too homogenous. And it's dated as soon as you finish, because next week the design world will be on to something else.

———————

A room that has only one thought, and one note, never works.

IN THIS HOUSE, ONE BIG ROOM SERVES AS KITCHEN, living room, and dining area. It's always a challenge when you have so many different functions in one space. How do you connect it all into a whole while still maintaining a sense of separation? It turns out that there are many ways of delineating space besides building a wall.

The kitchen is recessed into a large niche, which establishes its own perimeter. An island separates it from the rest of the room but does not close it off. In the living area, a high-backed sofa defines the seating group around the fireplace, setting it apart from the dining table. Each side of the room has equal weight. I painted an old chandelier pure white and put a Noguchi coffee table next to a traditional club chair to blur the distinction between antique and modern. The room is both. It's a 1940s house updated for today's more casual lifestyle.

Fabrics and furnishings make other subtle connections. The color of the wood on the dining table becomes the color of the cushions on the sofa. A large bay window outfitted with a window seat picks up the same tones. It's a place where the kids can throw themselves down and watch TV while the mother is cooking and the father is reading. A lot of activities take place here all at once. The family is together, but everyone can do their own thing.

BENJAMIN MOORE
STRATTON BLUE
HC-142

BENJAMIN MOORE
ASHWOOD GRAY
1654

BENJAMIN MOORE
PALLADIAN BLUE
HC-144

YEARS AGO, IN A HOUSE IN NATCHEZ, MISSISSIPPI, I saw a bookcase lined in gold leaf. I never forgot it. Here is my version, in a sitting room at a country club. I love the gold. It's completely unexpected, and it gives the whole room a glow. I covered the books in white paper to match the walls and shelves and finished off the composition with white cache-pots and white porcelain. It looks like something out of Paris in the 1930s. The room has a wonderful sense of softness, and drama.

ORIGINALLY, THIS OPEN ROOM WAS A KITCHEN THAT wasn't very big and a dining room that wasn't very big. But when we took down a wall and connected them into one large room, it became a space that was magical. There's always something special about dining in a kitchen. It feels very intimate to sit down in the same room where you prepare the food—like dining at that special table in a restaurant's kitchen. The bookcase and the picture ledge, against opposite walls, also give the room more warmth. It's not formal or stiff. It's a place where any guest would immediately feel like family.

149

It's easy to extract certain facts from a client—
I want to seat this many people for dinner, my
favorite color is blue. But what I'm really looking
for is emotion. What do you want your room
to feel like? Tell me what makes you happy, what
makes you sad. Then I'll take all those feelings
and try to translate them into an interior.

THIS DINING ROOM IS ALL ABOUT VERSATILITY.
It can seat twenty people, or four people, equally
comfortably. There are two square wood tables
mounted on open steel cubes, and they're both on
wheels. My clients can pull them together or
push them apart, depending on how many guests
they want to accommodate. The seating is also
very flexible, with two-seater sofas as well as chairs.
I carved a slot in the back of the sofa to add a
contemporary detail to a traditional shape. I love
slots. I always like to see slices of things. A wood
insert in the stone floor acts as a virtual carpet.

I DON'T LIKE SEEING THE BACK OF A SOFA WHEN I ENTER a room. So what's the solution? At the threshold of this living room, I added a half-round Swedish table and a parchment-covered screen. I like layering the visuals. First you focus on the table. Then you come around the screen and see the rest of the room. It's a delayed entrance, and that adds to the sense of discovery.

The best way for me to rethink an environment is to look at it in plan. That way I'm not distracted by the decoration or anything else that's already there. I can look at it in the abstract, as mass and volume, and focus on the skeleton of the space, not the surface. I can move from point to point and start to build from the inside out. It's my way of connecting with the space and starting to imagine what it could be.

IT'S NOT ALWAYS EASY TO GIVE A LARGE ROOM, with lots of furniture, a sense of flow. Here I chose to use a large curved sofa. The eye, caught by the curve, travels along the sofa to the window seat on the right. The two main seating areas are further connected by fabric—the same textile is used on the window seat and sofa. I like to cover an ottoman with durable leather, because that means you can put your feet up with no fears. And the round ottoman becomes the center of an even larger, room-size circle.

EXPAND
BHUTAN

I came to Bhutan because I wanted to hear the temple bells and smell the incense and breathe that fresh, sweet air you get when you're on the top of the world.

For the last ten years, I've been slowly exploring the Himalayas, trying to see something of the different countries carved out of this swath of high-altitude deserts, soaring mountains, and densely forested valleys. I've been to Leh on the northernmost tip of India, between Pakistan and Tibet. I've visited Kashmir, Nepal, Sikkim, Burma, and the eastern arm of India, Arunachal Pradesh. Even though these areas are not considered wealthy, the people seem to be utterly content, as though their capital cannot be measured in dollars. They can sit on the edge of a cliff just staring at the vista and look as if they're truly at rest.

The feeling I get in the Himalayas is something I have not experienced anywhere else. There's strength in this rough landscape. The mountains have a power that is indescribable. I think it's the closest we can get to heaven. Religion, in its various forms, has always fascinated me. The people of this region are predominantly Buddhist, and it seems a very peaceful way of life. I admire the instinctive spirituality. It's something I'm always trying to capture for myself and then transfer to my work.

Bhutan is still a kingdom, and for years it was closed to the West. Even now, only a certain number of tourists is allowed in each year. You have to apply for permission, and once you're approved, you must travel around the country in the company of an authorized guide. By keeping the number of visitors deliberately low, and making sure they stay a step away from the people, King Jigme Singye Wangchuck hoped to limit any outside influence. His overriding goal was to keep the traditional culture intact. He passed laws requiring his subjects to continue to wear the national dress. Yet at the same time, he was trying to expand education and provide health care. In 2006, he abdicated in favor of his son Khesar, and if the new king can lead the people of Bhutan (population estimates range from a million to twice that) into the modern world while still retaining their old-fashioned values, he will have pulled off a neat trick.

The airport in Paro is not even thirty years old. When I flew in on Druk Air, the sole national airline, only two planes came in each week. It looked as if we were landing in the middle of a grass field. I picked up my bags from the runway and was escorted into a ten-foot-square shack. A uniformed man behind a desk collected an entry fee of twenty dollars. Then I was introduced to my guide and driven to a hotel in Paro, where I spent the night. My itinerary was simple. I wanted to see the major monasteries, which form a chain of way stations along a sacred trail. Pilgrims used to spend months trekking up and down mountains to get from one to the next. But I had just a few weeks, so I was limited to those that were within striking distance of the road—the *only* road, euphemistically called the National Highway, which winds through the country from west to east and is barely one lane wide.

In the morning we got into the car and headed toward the first stop on my pilgrimage, the Taktshang Monastery. The name means Tiger's Nest, and it's probably Bhutan's most famous attraction. According to legend, Guru Rinpoche—the man who brought Buddhism to Bhutan in the eighth century—flew on the back of a tigress to this site, where he meditated in a cave for thirty days. The original temple was built around this cave in 1684. Fire has ravaged the place several times—a common fate in temples lit by flickering

yak-butter lamps—but it has always been rebuilt in exactly the same way. The monastery hugs the side of a sheer cliff, precariously perched half a mile above the floor of the Paro Valley.

We got as close as we could by car and then started hiking. Two and a half hours later, I'm panting. Any exercise in this thin air (the elevation is a mile and a half) requires a lot of energy. Meanwhile, the guide is blithely striding on ahead, then doubling back to offer water and encouragement. I consider myself very fit—I run or jump rope every day—yet I'm huffing and puffing. Where's my flying tigress when I need her? And we're still nowhere near the monastery. At least I have a good view of it from a small tea house on the trail, where we (and most other tourists) stop and call it quits. I'm so soaked with sweat that I peel off as many layers of clothing as I can and drape them in front of the fireplace to dry. After a long, leisurely cup of Darjeeling tea on the balcony, I'm ready to start back down. Along the pathway to the car, villagers have spread souvenirs out on blankets and call out, "Shopping! Shopping!" I bought an offering bowl made of copper and decorated with delicate gold medallions.

The road snakes south and then north, following the contours of the valley, before arriving in Thimphu, the capital—the only one in the world without a single traffic light. The road runs right through the center of town, past two-story buildings with shops. An all-purpose fabric store sells ready-made monk's robes, begging bowls, candles, and incense. Walk a little farther down the broad sidewalk and you'll find shops selling handmade paper and archery equipment. Archery is the national pastime. We kept passing people shooting arrows off into the distance as we drove along.

If you're dying for a hamburger, head straight to the Swiss Bakery, which also serves omelettes and Western-style pastries. Any foreigner in town seems to end up here for lunch, and the local office workers crowd in, too. It's a great place to sit and watch the world go by while you're sipping tea and devouring rum balls. My room at the Hotel Druk, purported to be the best in town, was sparsely furnished with a bed, a night table, and a desk—no competition for the view of the snow-capped Himalayas out the window. The breakfast buffet included Indian curries and dal as well as eggs.

In the morning, we set out for a small monastery, Chari Goemba, where a friend of my guide happened to be studying. When the road ended, we got out of the car and started meandering up a zigzag path through a rhododendron forest. When it rains, the water shoots down the path, leaving rocks and roots exposed, and those became our steps. If there's one thing I hate, it's climbing uphill, especially when sixty-year-old women carrying bundles of wood keep passing me. Forty-five minutes later, I'm cursing the fact that every monastery seems to be built on top of a mountain. But then we round a bend and walk into a courtyard with dogs and children running around. A young monk goes off in search of my guide's friend while I take a look at the main temple. It's a square building with massive wooden doors and hammered bronze knockers. The huge bronze hinges are engraved with dragons and seashells. An old man is gradually making his way around the perimeter on his knees, spinning the prayer wheels and sending the prayers out on the wind as he goes. That makes the little bells on top ring. A bell in the temple rings when the monks enter or leave, so the sound of bells seems to hover in the air.

The walls of the temple, inside and out, are made of mud. Whitewashed and painted with vibrant frescoes in turquoise, red, green, cobalt blue, and yellow, they depict the life of Buddha and various gods and demons. The colors fade quickly outdoors, and itinerant artists go from temple to temple, repainting the pictures. It's a shock to go from the bright sun to the darkness inside. I was examining the intricate paintings, all done for the glory and enhancement of Buddha, when the guide's friend arrived and asked if we wanted to visit his cell.

It's always fun to go behind the curtain and see the real thing. The monk took us into his small room, about six by ten feet; it had a mattress on the floor and a window with no glass, just open to the elements. A small wooden table held a bowl and some cups. There was a calendar on the wall with a photograph of the Eiffel Tower, and pictures of Buddha and the Dalai Lama were tacked up. He offered us tea made with yak milk. As soon as I finished one cup—Whew! I got it down!—he was refilling it. I found myself wondering

when the cup was last washed—keeping things clean here is not so easy. You have to bring a bucket up from the river. The bathroom in these places is a room cantilevered out from the hill with a hole in the floor. Very basic.

To be silent and still is very hard for me. I'm sitting there, my legs are crossed, and my bones are starting to ache. I know I don't want to go down that hill in the pitch dark, and he probably needs to go to prayers. And if I drink any more tea I'll have to visit that room with the hole in the floor. But he's so polite, nodding and smiling, and I keep smiling, and sipping my tea, as other monks peek in. Time is passing, but I tell myself it's okay. I'm expanding my horizons; enjoy the experience. Suddenly—nobody has to say it—we all simultaneously decide it's time to leave. I get up, thank him, and ask if I can take a picture of him. I write down his name and address, promising to send him a copy.

Our next big stop was the Trongsa monastery, which is located right in the middle of the country. As the road climbs over the Black Mountains, the high passes are lined with prayer flags—tall poles with long

vertical strips of fabric printed with prayers—fluttering in the wind and blowing the prayers off to heaven. We stopped in the Phobjika Valley to see the rare black-necked cranes that fly in from China to winter here. Our hotel was a simple farmhouse with no heat, just a pot-bellied stove where our host warmed rocks, which he picked up like hot potatoes and put in our beds. You nuzzle up to them like hot water bottles. I crawled out of bed while it was still dark because the cranes gather at sunrise. It's an unusual sight—all these strange creatures with feathery black collars around their long necks—but frankly I was more interested in the mist rising up off the grasses and creating a pearlescent pink floating blanket in the chill morning air as the sun rose. We returned to the farmhouse for breakfast, and then got back into the car.

The road became steeper and steeper, with hair-raising turns slicing into the side of the mountains, no guardrails, and barely enough room for two cars to pass. I quickly learned to sit on the side away from the precipice so I could avoid looking at the sheer drop to the valley below. We stopped for a picnic lunch at Chendebji Chorten, a whitewashed stone stupa with

eyes painted on all four sides. It was built in the eighteenth century to crush a demon who was tormenting the inhabitants—apparently it succeeded, because all is peaceful now. I sat on a boulder by a stream to eat my boiled eggs, and the only sound I heard was the water rushing by. Little shrines like this dot the countryside. People bring smooth black rocks, incised with prayers, and pile them up outside. It's an ongoing sculpture. The road snaked up and down, and as we drove through a cedar forest, a pack of mischievous brown monkeys pelted the car with fruit. Not quite the welcome I would expect, but finally there in the distance was Trongsa, with its rambling buildings and yellow roofs: the largest of the dzongs, or great fortress-monasteries along the pilgrim way.

My bathroom at the tourist lodge had a lovely window with no glass—and this was December. Showering was done with buckets of hot water. I've never seen such steam come off my body. It was invigorating, to say the least, like a Himalayan sauna. I had planned my trip in order to be here for a traditional festival, and I was eager to break in the Bhutanese outfit I had bought in Thimphu. The idea of me, six feet

tall, blending into a crowd of small, delicate Bhutanese was laughable, and no one would mistake me for a native, even in my gho—a long-sleeved white shirt and pants, layered with a vest and a black robe lined in bright yellow. I put it all on over my Chinese silk long johns (essential in this weather). Through my window I could faintly hear the music, and I went out and followed the crowd to a huge courtyard, where an enormous religious thangka, a painting four stories high, had been unfurled down the side of a building.

The dancers reenact different mythological stories. Men in long colorful skirts twirl and spin, wearing masks that represent different gods and demons and slashing swords at each other. When the bad guy gets whacked, all the kids laugh. Two or three hundred people sit on the ground, watching. More people hang out windows. Musicians are playing and gongs are ringing and singers are chanting. They are here to celebrate their religion and their history. Villagers come in from all over the countryside to stay at the dzong; everybody cooks and sleeps in one big room. It's a happening. Even after five hours of ritual dances, I didn't want to leave. I stayed for two more days, wandering

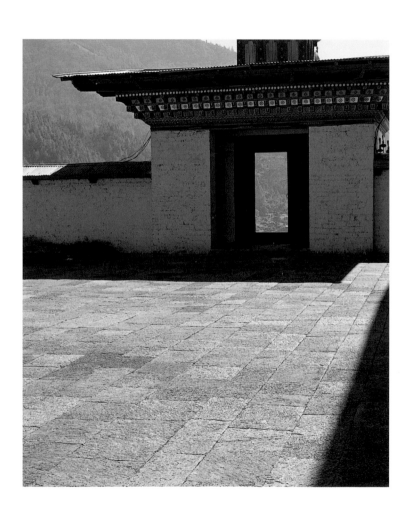

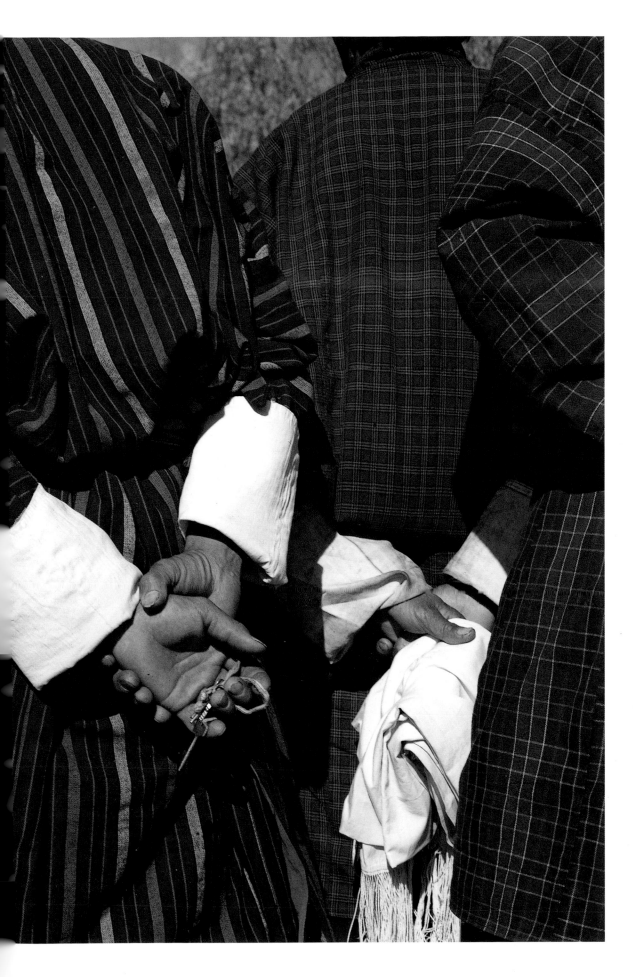

through the winding medieval streets, looking at shops and stalls selling herbs and amulets used to ward off evil spirits.

Then we got in the car to head to Bumthang, the last region I had time to see before flying home. The room in the little bungalow where I spent the night was heated only by a potbellied stove. As the temperature dropped, the embers went out. I tried to relight the stove, pouring in some more kerosene. By the time I found the matches in the dark, the kerosene had evaporated into gas, which ignited with an explosion as soon as I threw in the match. The next morning, my guide looked at me strangely when he saw the black stubs of my eyelashes. But I was focused on getting to our destination, Kurjey Lhakhang, one of the most sacred compounds in Bhutan. Guru Rinpoche meditated here centuries ago and left an imprint of his body in a cave, now incorporated into the monastery. The doorways are low, so you bow down as you enter and then emerge into a space over thirty feet high. Candles burn in yak butter lamps, and the only other light is from a window somewhere way up above. Against the wall is a huge gilded statue of Guru Rinpoche, two

stories tall, surrounded by a thousand smaller statues. As your eyes gradually get accustomed to the dimness, you notice the paintings on the walls. Colors emerge and the images come to life. The scent of incense lingers in the air.

I sat there for hours, in awe. I felt the power and the stillness of this sacred space that has been here for hundreds of years. The simplicity and the grandeur of the temple almost moved me to tears. I thought how lucky I was to be in this country, where time is not moving at the same pace it does in New York. Yet part of me was thinking that sooner or later these gentle people, with their windburned skin and long black hair and beautiful handmade clothes, are going to be altered as they interact more and more with the outside world. I looked around at my fellow worshippers and noticed the roughness of their hard-working hands as they sat and bowed, touching the floor with their foreheads in prayer. I found myself wishing that time would stand still. This country is so beautiful, just as it is.

EXPAND

BEFORE & AFTER

You don't choose your relatives, and you don't choose your clients: they choose you. Sometimes, as with Jyll and John, it's a perfect match. This couple had come together later in life, meeting at the newspaper where they both worked. To be part of a romance between charming, intelligent, and stimulating people, even if peripherally, was a pleasure.

Their interests couldn't have been more different. Jyll was very into her house and came with a lot of furniture collected over the years, crusty antiques in pale, pretty colors with an unpretentious flea market quality. Her apartment was dainty, with a distinctly feminine point of view. Her mother had been an interior designer, and Jyll had grown up with a sense of style.

John, on the other hand, had never thought about style. He was the kind of newspaperman that you see in movies, for whom a house is a place to get together with the guys to play cards, smoke cigars, and then go to sleep. He was a big burly fellow, and design was not in his vocabulary. He didn't care what went into the new apartment as long as he had a big, comfortable place to sit with his feet up.

The apartment they bought, a loft in Manhattan's Meatpacking District, still had traces of the original shell—cast-iron beams, columns, and an exposed brick wall. But it had been converted into a more conventional apartment with three bedrooms and honey-colored oak floors. The ceilings were relatively high. Light poured through the windows. For a lot of people, it would have been perfect. But I hate brick, and I hate honey-colored floors. Maybe forty years ago it worked, but now it feels aesthetically worn out, a visual cliché. Also, the living room was awkwardly long and narrow.

Jyll instinctively knew that the place would benefit from some rethinking, but she had never hired a designer before. As much as she admired my work, she was a little apprehensive of what it would be like to work with somebody with a strong point of view. Her main worry was that I would rob her of her individuality by putting my stamp on their home. I explained that working together would instead be about discovering what they liked and what they needed.

INTERVIEW NOTES
GENERAL

Colorless but not monotone

Textured fabrics and stone

LIVING ROOM

Seating for 8–12 people

Combination of loose and tight cushions

Deep seating

Television

DINING ROOM

Seating for 8 people with expansion for holidays

Informal without tablecloths or place mats

Blending of chairs (leather and metal, etc.)

KITCHEN

Kitchen should disappear from living room

Seating for 2 for conversation during food preparation

Overhead lighting

MASTER BEDROOM

King-size bed, no footboard

Two night tables

Lounge chair

Wall-to-wall carpet or area rug

Soft window treatment with blackout lining

LIBRARY

Seating for 6 people

Window treatment with blackout shades

Built-in bookcase for 500–1,000 books

Television

When I embark on a relationship with a client, I always proceed with caution. For example, when I first walked through the apartment with the couple, I did not announce how I felt about the brick wall and the floors. Instead, I listened to their comments, and I asked them what they liked and what they didn't like. I try to see the space through my clients' eyes. I'm also trying to absorb something about their personalities, even when they have little to say. I want to see how they relate to objects, and to each other. What's their body language: are they stiff, relaxed, playful? You don't want to give an uptight person a very casual room, because they're going to feel out of place.

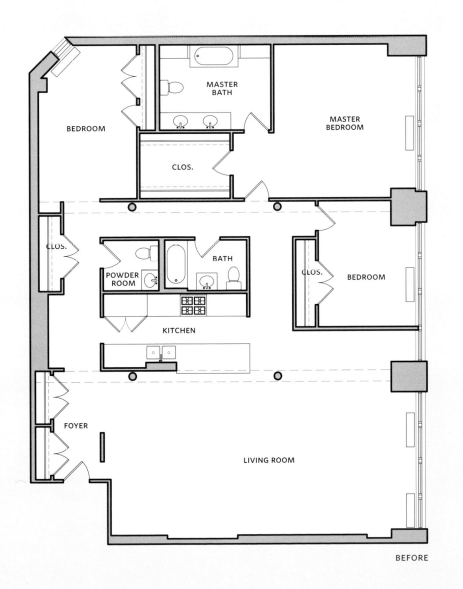

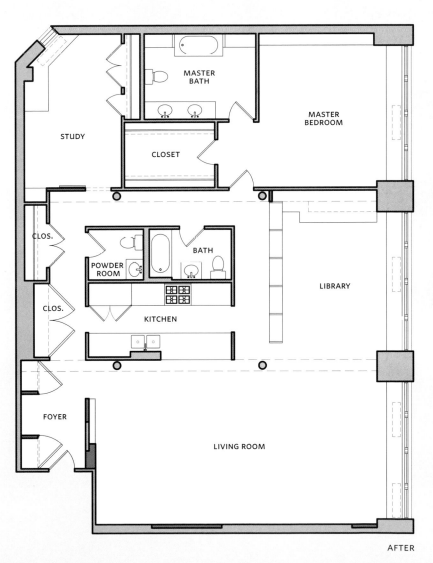

BEFORE

AFTER

THE WALK-THROUGH is an interesting moment. You're trying to figure out what's going to make the space sing, weigh the cost against the budget, and at the same time make a connection with the client, whom you're still trying to get to know. Jyll's and John's reactions were revealing. He thought the apartment was just fine. Clearly, he would rather read a book than deal with decorating. Jyll was more focused. She thought the brick wall, on just one side of the living room, cut the space in two and made it feel schizophrenic. She was right. I didn't know quite what to do with the brick yet, but I was sure it had to be neutralized. The long narrow shape of the room was also a problem, but I instantly recognized the solution. The wall between the guest bedroom and the living room had to come down. Normally in a Manhattan apartment, you don't eliminate a room for fear of reducing the resale value, but when I suggested opening up the guest bedroom and making it more of a den, she was excited. It would break that bowling-alley quality and reveal more of the run of windows, expanding the space.

As for the honey-colored floors, Jyll didn't like them either (ah ha! we think alike!); she felt they looked too "rental." Should we bleach them, paint them white, or stain them very dark? My sense was that bleaching them would be best. It would carry the light and soften the space.

She liked the open kitchen because she could cook for the two of them and not feel isolated. But they were planning to entertain a lot, and she wanted the option of closing it off for business dinners, when caterers would be manning the stove. The other thing Jyll wanted was a proper foyer. As it was, visitors stepped through the front door and saw the living room right away through a large gap in a partition wall. There was no sense of arrival.

It's at this point—after I've gathered information and feelings and had the clients fill out my questionnaire, pinning down their requirements—that I retreat to the drafting board. I want to conceptualize the design as a whole. I have learned that if you approach the job in a piecemeal way, it's going to look piecemeal. It's better when everything is designed all at once. Otherwise it's hard to achieve visual continuity.

I start by dealing with the architecture, looking for structural changes. That way, when I go to the next step, creating furniture plans, I already have an altered space in my mind. It's like a puzzle. You're trying to see how the parts will fit. Working with tracing paper, I start looking at different furniture arrangements, even before I have any idea of what the exact furniture is going to be. I visualize elevations in my mind, imagining how the furniture will play in the space. I work with blocks of shapes—here we need a chair, this should be a sofa. When I get to an arrangement that seems right and takes care of the clients' needs, and also has something unique about it, I stop.

The next step is to figure out the materials and colors. I've balanced the forms in the abstract, and have a good idea of which elements will probably be new and which could be antiques. I've also taken photographs and measured all the pieces that the clients want to incorporate into their new home. It takes me weeks and weeks to refine the design, and by the time I'm ready to present the scheme, I am fully committed.

Then, if there's an objection from the clients, there are a few ways to deal with it. One, I could give in without question. Two, I could try to explain to the client why I've done what I've proposed. Many times people don't understand the aesthetic reasoning, and if you can articulate it in a clear and

INSTALLATION: LIVING ROOM

intelligent way, you have a better chance of putting your thoughts across. Three, I could scream and shout and kick and cry. Frankly, this doesn't work. If you say you love it, they can say they don't. Then it's, I'm right and you're wrong, which is not the most effective psychology to utilize.

———————

You want a room to have a long life. You can't be thinking of it as right now. You have to think of it in an expansive way, beyond period. You take what you like from today, from yesterday, and from what's coming tomorrow.

BEFORE: LIVING ROOM AND FOYER

CONSTRUCTION: LIVING ROOM AND FOYER

Our strategy to liberate space is to knock walls down, but there are plenty of other strategies. You can eliminate doors between rooms and take the openings all the way up to the ceiling to create a sense of flow.

LUCKILY, JYLL, JOHN, AND I all agreed on the structural changes, and we went straight to my favorite part of any job—demolition. I love seeing walls go down and others go up. The raw energy of transformation is to me the most electric part of a job. Details begin to coalesce. The vision starts to expand. Usually the architectural surgery is subtractive, but in this apartment we also added. By extending the partition wall at the entry, we shaped a simple foyer. Narrowing the original gap gave the space a new fourth wall and a sense of enclosure. It became a room. Now you get only a quick flash of the windows as you walk in, a glimpse but not much more. And when you are sitting in the living room, you can no longer see the front door—much more gracious. We added a picture ledge to the partition on the living room side, for artwork.

Small changes can make a big difference. The hollow-core light wood closet doors on the other side of the foyer looked flimsy. We switched to solid core doors, which feel more substantial, detailing them so that the doors blended into the larger wall. The overall impression was stronger, more architectural. Between the two closets, I created a niche for a piece of furniture. It was an opportunity to set the tone and spirit of the apartment, and I chose something I had found years ago—a nineteenth-century oak artist's table with a fold-up easel, perfect for displaying a painting or photograph. It's a charming piece, with a drawer for brushes and a little side shelf. I designed a delicate klismos bench to sit in front of it. Overhead, one of my clients' light fixtures, an unusual starburst chandelier, completes the space.

NOW TO THE KITCHEN. Both corners were open to the living area, and the right end had a breakfast bar where you'd sit with a cup of coffee facing into the space. I walled in the left corner so you couldn't see into the kitchen from the new foyer and shaved off the overhanging counter to establish a flat plane. Then we built a white partition wall that slides on a track back and forth across the kitchen. Rolled to the right, it closes off the opening; rolled to the left, it blends into the solid kitchen wall, opening the kitchen to the living area. You can have it both ways.

I wanted the apartment to be changeable, to take on different configurations with different uses. We did a long wooden table on wheels; in the dining room, it could be used as a server. The table is low enough so that it also works as a movable bench. On either side, it has a stainless-steel footrest. You could park it in front of the breakfast bar and sit and have a conversation with the cook. I scaled it so that it would be large and solid enough to make an architectural impact. It holds its own in the big space.

BEFORE: KITCHEN

CONSTRUCTION: KITCHEN

CONSTRUCTION: KITCHEN

THE OTHER CHALLENGE was the brick wall. You could sheetrock over it. You could paint it white. Or you could paint it white and hang a sheer curtain over it. The curtain had the benefit of bringing a softer dimension to the space, plus a sense of romance, which appealed to Jyll. I thought John might be a harder sell, but his reaction was, "Whatever you like, honey." I made the curtains out of a linen gauze, which we hung floor to ceiling across the entire length of the living room. The light played across the surface and animated the whole wall. I tailored the curtains to go around the sprinkler pipes, which reinforced the industrial feeling of the space.

In a room snow-blinded by white, colors can float. White is the first thought, the first gesture. It's the start, and I like rooms that have a start that doesn't come to an end.

BEFORE: LIVING ROOM

CONSTRUCTION: LIVING ROOM

INSTALLATION: LIVING ROOM

INSTALLATION: LIVING ROOM

MANY OF THE INTERIORS I design feature large-scale mirrors. Over the years, they have gotten bigger and bigger, and further and further away from the conventional sense of a mirror. They have become more environmental, like architectural doors that suggest a space beyond, reflecting windows and pieces of furniture. They fool the eye about the actual shape of the room. I decided to put an overscaled, floor-to-ceiling mirror in front of the curtains. When you enter the space, it doubles the apparent number of windows in the room, reflecting more light and breaking up the rectangular quality.

But there are certain limitations when you're designing a large mirror in Manhattan. You have to make sure it will fit in the elevator and through the doorway. What I ended up doing here was creating grids within the mirror itself, dividing it into separate pieces of glass that could be assembled, along with the frame, inside the apartment. It can take hours to fit the sheets of glass and balance them correctly (torquing a mirror even slightly can break it). An oversized mirror is not cheap, but for a controlled amount of money you can bring an enormous sense of drama into a space. A good piece of art might create the same drama, but at a far greater price.

One easy way to give a room more depth is with a large-scale mirror. A mirror widens a room and gives you fractured glimpses of the furniture. It frames a still life that keeps changing as you move through. A mirror gives the illusion of even more space, especially when you're seeing it on the diagonal. It stretches the space.

BENJAMIN MOORE
CLAY
1034

BENJAMIN MOORE
OAKWOOD
MANOR
1095

BENJAMIN MOORE
COTTON BALLS
OC-122

FABRICS: LIVING ROOM

RENDERING: LIVING ROOM AND DINING AREA

OUR ONLY DISAGREEMENT WAS over the furniture plan. I originally thought that we would use a curved sofa in front of the mirror, which would escape the loft's dominating sense of straight lines, and an L-shaped banquette for the dining area. But in both these cases, all my rationales could not convince Jyll (and there was no point in screaming). It just didn't work for her. She was more comfortable with straight lines. She also wanted a more familiar seating arrangement around the dining table. It's very hard when you think you've come up with the best solution to think of another best solution, but sometimes you have to design to a client's comfort level.

The curved sofa became an L-shaped sofa, and I balanced out the hard surfaces in the room by choosing a deep, low piece with billowing cushions and leather throw pillows, which echo two silvery leather armchairs. I designed a coffee table made of pickled oak, which was sturdy enough to invite John to put up his feet. I like generous coffee tables with big surfaces because they can carry tablescapes, which give a room detail and character. We started out with a Murano vase and antique Italian candlesticks, but you should always rotate the objects to keep the room alive. Against the window in the background, I set an old Indian window with delicate marble tracery, which diffuses the light.

BEFORE: DINING AREA

AS FOR THE DINING TABLE, WITHOUT THE BANQUETTE, it no longer belonged to the wall. I moved the table into the center of the space and surrounded it with different types of chairs, as at a dinner party when you want to mix your guests. I picked three slip-covered tub chairs and three caned Burmese chairs. The combination of upholstered and framed chairs brought a focus to the center of the room, because that's where the visual conversation was. I confirmed the point by hanging an outsized custom-made rectangular white lampshade over the dining table. It almost creates a room in itself.

When you say the word *expand*, what comes to mind is the body's lungs. When you breathe in and fill them up with air, they expand. The oxygen you take in keeps you alive. In the same way, a room has to be always taking in fresh air. It cannot be stuck in one period if you want it to stay alive. You have to keep infusing it with oxygen.

BEFORE: LIVING ROOM

CONSTRUCTION: LIBRARY

CONSTRUCTION: LIBRARY

THE FORMER GUEST ROOM, which we were merging into the living room, would function as a flex space— a television area, library, and guest room. But how was I going to make it fulfill all those different functions? First, to define the area, and give it the potential for some privacy, I designed a floor-to-ceiling gridded bookcase. Deep enough to be used on both sides, it has an architectural scale and look. The bookcase has no back and effectively became a screen defining the television room from the corridor leading to the master bedroom. Jyll uses the side facing the kitchen for cookbooks, and the other side has become their library. You can see through the structure to the windows, expanding the view from the living room and kitchen, and the open grid brings natural light into the hallway and kitchen.

Perhaps because of my interest in photography, I've noticed that you can play with the depth of field in a project to expand space. I'm fascinated by the architecture of Versailles or the gardens at the Alhambra or that long entrance pool and walkway in front of the Taj Mahal, all for the same reason: they end in a strong focal point.

Inside, I designed banquette seating that could double as a queen-size bed for guests and hung more gauze curtains. These could be pulled shut, for privacy. I bleached the floor, as in the rest of the apartment, and installed an area rug to give the room some visual separation. Four framed artworks hang over the back of the banquette, keeping the eye low and the space intimate. This was the kind of spot where you'd want to curl up with a book. In front, there's a big round nineteenth-century Swedish drop-leaf table; with overflow party guests, it can become another dinner setting. When the table is at ease, the half-round dropped leaves look very geometric, like a piece of contemporary art. With a Chinese chair and African stool, the room blends different cultures. The simple white background handles the mixture easily.

IN THE MASTER BEDROOM, I faced the bed toward the window, floating it out from a folded white metal screen. Now when you enter the room, you don't confront the back of a bed but focus on a sunburst mirror hung on the screen. You then come around the screen and discover the room. First you see a long antique pharmaceutical cabinet of drawers, from Jyll's former apartment. If you squint, its gritty texture looks a little like a minimalist painting. A picture rail hovers over that, holding paintings, pictures, and objects she's collected over the years. All her quirky, unusual things acquire a sense of strength against the clean white backdrop. The sleigh bed, which I designed years ago for Henredon, has a strong but graceful presence of its own and floats on a taupe, cut-wool carpet that grounds the space and acts as an island organizing the furniture. Jyll and John like to read in bed, and this bed, with its big tufted headboard, feels like an environment of its own.

I like the extravagance of generous night tables, a great reading light, a comfortable sofa or chair, and soft colorations that flatter skin tones.

BENJAMIN MOORE
LIGHT PEWTER
1464

BENJAMIN MOORE
1544

BENJAMIN MOORE
GLASS SLIPPER
1632

BENJAMIN MOORE
1586

FABRICS: BEDROOM

I HAVE A REGULAR PROCEDURE FOR MY JOBS. After the design is done—architecture, furniture, materials— I present all the items to the clients, so that the complete job can be billed and ordered. Then it takes seventeen to twenty weeks to produce it: construction, finishing, painting, and furniture fabrication. The approvals give you the freedom to focus on the job as a whole, so that you're not going back again and again to fill in the blanks and losing your train of thought. Ordering everything at one time also gives you better control of the time frame.

Once the job is rolling, I check in on the site and visit the cabinetmakers and upholsterers to make sure it's all being done according to plan. When the shell of the apartment or house is done, and the furniture is built, we start the installation. First, the carpets and window treatments arrive, and then the furniture. I generally ask my clients to leave so that my crew and I can put it all together. Seeing it incomplete is like tasting a meal before it's cooked— you're not getting the full flavor. I've found that it's a big mistake to let the clients peek in on an installation before it's all finished. A piece may look too big or too small when it's not surrounded by everything else that is meant to go around it. Doing an installation is like getting dressed to go out. You keep adjusting slowly, and everything starts to settle into its own place. That process of adjustment works best when the clients aren't there. It's my time in the delivery room, and I don't like an audience. When the apartment is done, as a finishing touch, I bring in flowers, accessories, candles, plants, the works. Who wants to see a show in rehearsal, before the curtain is ready to go up?

The hand-off, when the apartment passes from you to them, is always an emotional moment. The number one supreme reaction is tears. If they cry, that's a 10. And sometimes you hear, "Wow, this is way more than I envisioned." That always surprises me. You have just spent days and weeks explaining every item—showing pictures, drawing renderings, gathering fabric samples. For me, it reinforces the fact that it's vital to be very clear every step of the way, since most people are hiring you precisely because they lack the capability to visualize. It's always so satisfying when they're pleased. What's interesting is that 90 percent of the time, they immediately feel as if they belong there.

In the case of John and Jyll, the project had a very happy ending. The transformation of the apartment gave John a whole new appreciation of design. And I was particularly gratified to see how much Jyll liked it. She assumed possession of it immediately and uncorked a bottle of champagne. I could see she felt comfortable. Her objects had been used. She had participated in creating this space. She poured out three brimming glasses.

After the unveiling, when I finally leave, I understand how actors feel after they've performed onstage—exhausted but exhilarated. You've worked for five and a half months to get to this moment, and now it's over. You walk away. But a few months after this installation, I was lucky enough to be invited to John and Jyll's wedding. When they said their vows, I got teary-eyed. The whole experience was definitely a 10.

EXPAND
ENVIRONMENTS

Besides playing with a room's physical boundaries, you can expand a room by stretching its non-physical boundaries. I like rooms that are not caught in time, rooms that will have the same impact in ten years that they have now. When there's a mixture of furniture from different periods and places, you don't know when the room was done.

——————

ARCHITECTURE HAS BEEN DEFINED AS THE ART OF THE possible. Sometimes more is possible, sometimes less. My first impulse for this turn-of-the-century apartment in a building on Central Park West was to open it all up and merge the living and dining rooms into one large, expanded space. The dining room had a view of Central Park, and if I knocked down a wall, you would be able to see it from the living room as well. But my clients did not want to do any major work in an apartment that they had just bought, already renovated. I had to adapt to what was already there. Both husband and wife were very precise about what they liked and did not like. They were familiar with my work and wanted a soft blue palette, dark woods, and a beautiful rug on the living room floor.

I think every space has its pros and cons. In this case, a fake fireplace in the middle of the short wall of the rectangular living room had forced the previous owners to orient the furniture away from the view. The fireplace was easy to remove, but what should I do with the off-center window on the same wall? The best way to camouflage it was to hang curtains along the whole wall, making it look like there were more windows underneath. No one is really fooled, but the block of fabric does accentuate the apparent width of the space while balancing the off-center window.

BENJAMIN MOORE
OLYMPIC
MOUNTAINS
971

BENJAMIN MOORE
RIVIERA AZURE
822

BENJAMIN MOORE
INDIAN WHITE
OC-88

BENJAMIN MOORE
BLANCHED
ALMOND
1060

The asymmetry gave me the freedom to create an unusual seating arrangement with a curved sofa. Putting the sofa in the corner expanded the sense of space. The curve of the sofa echoed the curve of the table I picked for the center of the room, which helped move the eye around the space. It's a strange analogy, but the eye is like a ricocheting pinball. You want to lead it through space, like Caravaggio leads you through his paintings with color and shape and light. Here, the first thing you see as you walk into the room is the round pedestal table. The eye follows the curve, and then shoots off to the other curve of the sofa. By putting the seating group in the corner, I galvanized the space, leading the eye to the farthest point. I wanted to break the box of the room. It all started with that English Edwardian pedestal table, which kept the area between the living room and dining room from becoming a mere passageway. If you see a blank space as your first experience of a room, it sets the wrong atmosphere and mood, and you will never quite recover.

I like to design a room and then find a rug that works with the space, which is contrary to how most people operate. They start with the rug, and then match all the fabrics to it. I prefer to think of a rug as a piece of art. It's like a painting on the floor, and I don't believe in matching your upholstery to your paintings. If a beautiful antique rug is not in the budget, I'd rather do sisal or a plain wool carpet. They're good, natural materials that can hold their own in any space.

The energy comes from the eclectic mix of furniture. The pedestal table stands next to a three-armed midcentury modern lamp. In the seating area, there's a great Ethiopian chair, a little Indian child's chair that holds books, and a Chinese trunk, plus the sofa and ottoman and club chairs we designed ourselves. As always, accessories count, like the old candlesticks and the Indonesian masks, all the more interesting because they're menacing rather than pretty. That adds edge.

But the most unusual gesture is the painting hung on top of the curtain. After registering the wall of curtains, you zero in on the piece of art. It gives the eye something to rest on, and it's rather mysterious. You get the sense that the painting is just floating in midair.

203

SOMETIMES IT'S INTERESTING TO TILT A ROOM OFF-center. Here, there were a couple of reasons for placing the dining table to one side. First, the clients didn't want to overcommit the room to dining, since they would also be using the table for work. So we avoided the dinner-only connotation you get from a central table with a group of identical chairs. To emphasize the shift, I hung the chandelier off-center, on the same side. The second reason to move the table was that I wanted to draw more attention to the beautiful bay window, which I furnished with cushions and pillows, making it into an informal window seat. Now there are two seating areas in the room, one around the window and the other around the table. It's a new balance of power.

Usually a fireplace snaps you right back to symmetry, but I threw the mantel off by placing a small Rembrandt etching to one side. On the other side is a collection of antique Thai bronze mirrors. You see all the objects more clearly this way. Anything placed in the center of a mantel tends to die, or at least lose its energy. You stop seeing it after a while.

The floor is stained a dark ebony, to give it more depth, and the walls are painted white. There's something very powerful about the contrast of dark and light.

Colors have names: red, blue, green. But white is not a color. It's almost unidentifiable. You can't pin it down. It evaporates. It's a zero. White is void. Staying within its indeterminate range expands the whole sense of space, because white evaporates boundaries.

BENJAMIN MOORE
LEMON SOUFFLÉ
331

BENJAMIN MOORE
PALE AVOCADO
2146-40

BENJAMIN MOORE
TEN GALLON HAT
1210

BENJAMIN MOORE
INTERCOASTAL
GREEN
672

WHEN YOU DESIGN FOR A CLIENT, YOU PUT YOUR
career on the line. When you design for a friend, you
put your life on the line. Your closest buddy could
become your nemesis, especially if he has a one-
bedroom apartment in an awkward shape that's very
difficult to work with.

My friend Preston Bailey has an apartment in a
former commercial building in Murray Hill. It
was blessed with enormous windows and incredible
light, but the layout was odd and the rooms felt
tight. Preston is a man of sweeping gestures. He's
in the entertainment industry and organizes special
events, spectacular occasions for clients around
the world. He's accustomed to spaces that go up
with a bang and come down four days later. The
advantage to working with someone like Preston is
that he's adventurous. Approaching his space,
I was able to read his character, which was theatrical,
and create a setting that suited him. He wanted
this apartment to have a lot of drama and pizzazz.
He had lived there for twenty-six years, and for most
of that time, the apartment had been white. Now
he wanted color, and not just in a subtle way. He

wanted exuberance. We painted the walls an
unusual greeny-yellow and brought in teal blue and
chartreuse with the fabrics and upholstery.

I couldn't wait to knock down the wall between
the bedroom and living room to make one big space.
It would expand the living area, lengthen the run
of windows, and increase the amount of light.
Preston was cool with the idea as long as he would
still be able to close off the bedroom for privacy.

At the far end of the new, enlarged room, I
raised the bed on a platform and created an overscaled
Parsons-style, stainless-steel frame around it, which
filled the whole space. We upholstered the box spring
and mattress so that the bed could double as a large
sofa for entertaining. The bed no longer really looks
like a bed but has acquired an almost regal presence,
like a stage set. The steel frame turned it into a
modern version of a Chinese opium bed. And just as
I had promised, I layered two sets of curtains, one
sheer and the other opaque, so Preston could close off
the bed when he wanted privacy. The sheer curtain
is the same lime yellow as the walls, and the opaque
curtain is a blue that echoes the teal of the carpet.

I added a deeper note to the palette at the opposite end of the room with bronze leather upholstery on the ottoman and two floor-to-ceiling mirrors framed in coppery mirror. The mirrors blur the boundaries of the space and make it feel even bigger. The sofa is upholstered in the same fabric as the bed, so the two relate to each other across the length of the space.

I thought the furniture should be strong, tranquil, and timeless, and found some elegant Chinese pieces that were minimal enough to bridge the gap between classic and modern. Just a few pieces—an altar table, a pair of Ming chairs, and a geometric screen—set the tone and give the contemporary apartment a different dimension.

The geometries of the apartment and the furniture are angular and rectangular, so I added a few more elements to soften the lines. Rustic Burmese wooden wheels bring in a primitive quality. I placed them on metal pedestals behind the sofa, to fill up a space that is normally difficult to occupy. Behind the bed, a pair of antlered wooden heads tell another story. These figures, according to Burmese myth, are protective spirits. I love how they're silhouetted against the light from the window.

Whenever I went slightly over the line in favor of drama, Preston loved it. I wasn't dealing with the restraint a regular client brings to the table. When you're designing a space, you have to take into account the person who lives there. If you create an overwhelming environment for the wrong personality, the space eats them up. No danger of that here. Preston stands out, even in this striking apartment.

THIS GUEST HOUSE IN NANTUCKET WAS ONCE USED for storage. The wood interiors were dark, and you didn't want to go there. My client was considering knocking it down.

I thought, Wait a minute. It isn't a perfect space, but it has a sense of the past. It also had a quirky charm, especially in the small second-floor loft, with angles angling off angles on the ceiling. The first floor had a nice bank of windows, but it was weighed down by dark wooden beams. The architectural elements didn't show to their best advantage.

Finally the client agreed to keep it, but he didn't want to spend a lot of money redoing it. So we recycled an old wicker sofa left behind by the previous owner and painted it white. We ordered inexpensive pieces from catalogs like Crate & Barrel and Wisteria to fill in the blanks. But the biggest change occurred when we painted the whole space white. It just brought the place to life. Walls and beams were suddenly unified. White transformed a dingy shack into a romantic hideaway.

I wanted it to have an irreverent quality, and I think the large tin urn on a pedestal, from the Wisteria catalog, contributes to that. It's a nice juxtaposition to the Lucite chairs. The big bulbous baluster table offers another jump in scale. It's fun to be in this room. When it's not being used by guests, the daughters fight to stay there.

BENJAMIN MOORE
DILL PICKLE
2147-40

BENJAMIN MOORE
VALENTINE'S DAY
2077-60

Bringing a large-scale piece into a small room can alter your perception of its size. It tricks the mind into thinking the space is bigger than it really is. This certainly works in the bedroom upstairs, where a queen-size bed fills the room. Bold apple-green upholstery makes it stand out even more. The sleigh bed came straight from a catalog, and it brings a sense of softness and sophistication to an otherwise plain room.

Mounting a flat-screen TV to the wall worked very well in such a tight space. The pert little chair just beneath it has a 1950s quality. The splashy pattern is a big departure for me, but who could resist? It made me smile.

If you're using tiles of stone or ceramic, large-scale squares expand the space. Reflections, even the vague reflections of lacquered walls and ceilings, double the height or width of a room.

WHEN A BATHROOM HAS NATURAL LIGHT, IT TAKES on a sense of brightness and cleanliness. But often a bathroom has no windows, and you have to create your own glow.

Here I did it by doing two walls in frosted glass, which shimmers. Then, to bring natural light into the space, I fit a small skylight between the rafters of the roof. The well is much wider than the actual skylight, which makes it look larger, and the sides of the well are slanted, so the light coming in spreads and expands. The light washes the whole back wall and seems to come from an unknown source, which makes it more intriguing.

I did the other two walls and floor in a light limestone. Instead of a shower door, we designed a floating wall of glass set in a channel in the floor and ceiling—there's no frame to interrupt the flow of space. Curbs around a shower likewise stop the flow, so we dropped the shower floor two inches to eliminate the need for a curb and create the illusion of a continuous floor. Three equally spaced Bega luminaires add more light at night.

All the fixtures and details send the same message of openness and airiness. An Indian antique marble bench, a Philippe Starck shower head, a linear drain, and a column that holds the shower hose all simplify the look. Outside the shower in the bath area, a wood countertop holds a stainless-steel bowl with an open shelf and cabinet below.

When the bathroom door is closed and the lights inside are on, the bathroom is a glowing cube of frosted glass. It's as much fun to see from the outside as from the inside.

IT MAY SEEM COUNTERINTUITIVE, BUT THE CHINESE say that if you want to make a space look bigger, divide it. And that's what I ended up doing in this kitchen. The space was quite long and wide, and I built a long, tall row of cabinets to define a kitchen area and a breakfast area. I wanted people in the kitchen to look through to the breakfast table, and I wanted natural light from the breakfast room to come into the kitchen.

The traditional paned windows of the house cued the geometry of the cabinets. I designed them as a grid, with glass doors on both sides. You can see through the grid, yet it fractures the view. It reminds me of a Chuck Close painting—if you look at it up close, you see that everything is made up of a grid, and each little section becomes part of the total picture. All the fragments add up to a portrait, and in this case, a room.

I added the cabinets for storage, but there was also an aesthetic motive. I like the layered effect that you get when you see through the plates and the crystal to the room beyond. Looking through that grid and seeing the Saarinen white molded-plastic chairs pulled up to an eighteenth-century country table felt like a great way to play with the space, and also with the sense of time. Modern mixes with traditional. And it happens in the kitchen as well. The island is supported by traditional baluster legs, paired with very modern stools. I stained the terra-cotta floors dark to ground the space and give the floor a more solid, monolithic quality in contrast to the airy white grid.

BENJAMIN MOORE
GOLDEN
ORCHARDS
329

NAPOLEON WAS SHORT, BUT HIS AURA MADE HIM
look ten feet tall. I wanted to give this small guest
room a much bigger aura, something to counteract
not only its size but also the dullness of a tight,
conventional space.

My strategy was to change the subject, to draw
attention away from the size of the room and direct
it to an inventive detail, something unexpected like
that pure white grid. It functions as a headboard
but it's not a solid mass, so it doesn't stop the room.
And I inserted it ten inches from the wall, which
most people wouldn't have done, fearing that it
would shortchange the space. But that intriguing
little gap creates a whole new plane and another
dimension, which seems to expand the room.

I layered the back wall with canary yellow
shades. In an otherwise white room, the yellow is a
big surprise. It makes the white grid really pop—
it almost looks like a trellis in the sun. It's fun to
challenge the obvious, to look for ways to fool
and surprise the eye. A small room doesn't have
to be treated in a small way.

A grid is an architectural way of bringing in
pattern. It's basically the idea of a trellis, but in a
more modern version. It can deliver a strong
impact without much expense. It doesn't have
to be an antique Chinese window; it can be a
homemade wooden grid. I'll often set mirrors
within the grid to give a reflection that isn't
obvious. That's a very different thing from hanging
a mirror on a wall. You're bringing in more texture
and introducing another geometric element.

BENJAMIN MOORE
ST. ELMO'S FIRE
362

BENJAMIN MOORE
BURMUDA
TURQUOISE
728

I OFTEN DO WHITE FLOORS, WALLS, AND CEILINGS because they erase the boundaries of a room and open the space. But the opposite turns out to work just as well. While white evaporates the edges of a room, a very dark shade absorbs and obscures them. But the results are the same: both expand the perception of space. Choosing one or the other sets up a very different mood—you have to select which emotion you want in the room. White is extroverted and dark is introverted. I don't like rooms that are painted some middle-of-the-road shade. I like them bright or I like them dark. Maybe it has to do with clarity of intent. I want a full emotion, not something that goes only halfway.

In this living room, I covered the walls in a dark teal strié, which makes them seem to disappear. At the same time, the windows open the room and push your eye out. You look beyond the structure to the garden outside. And the grid of windows casts dramatic patterns of shifting light.

I wanted curves on the furniture to play against that linear grid. Everything is upholstered in tones of teal blue with bright chartreuse accents. That contrast of color makes the room feel more modern. A teal carpet erases the floor as a boundary in the same way the teal fabric erases the walls. The darkness is inky and dense, and then that glorious Miró painting seems to jump off the wall. It's lighthearted and bright. The Jeff Koons ceramic dog waits by the chair and adds its own bit of whimsy.

I tend to approach master bedrooms for married couples as the woman's domain. Men get the feeling that they have been invited into a lady's boudoir. He enters the embrace of feminine softness. He's seduced and caressed by gentle fabrics and colors. A man should be engulfed, but not feel as if he is out of place.

———————

I like beds to be soft, to convey warmth. And I like upholstered beds. Who wants to bump against a hard edge? There's something about an upholstered sleigh bed that feels so glamorous to me. It's like a gondola, transporting you into another realm. It draws you in and cocoons you.

WHEN CEILINGS GET TOO HIGH, THEY DEHUMANIZE A space. To camouflage the humongous height of the sixteen-foot ceiling in this bedroom, I erected a screen behind the bed. Stopping three feet below the ceiling, it lowers the virtual lid on the room, creating a more human scale and some sense of intimacy. The folding screen gives the room a new surface, which I decorated with a graphic criss-cross of ribbons—grosgrain over taupe silk. It looks a little like a trellis, and adds texture. The new pattern, moving in and out on the folded panels, animates the space. A ten-foot-high mirror reflects the windows, doubling the light and the view and affirming the virtual horizon line established by the screen.

BENJAMIN MOORE
372

BENJAMIN MOORE
SILVER BELLS
1458

BENJAMIN MOORE
1466

BENJAMIN MOORE
HARVEST TIME
186

I THINK YOU SHOULD SEE THE BED STRAIGHT ON WHEN you enter a bedroom. Then you're seeing the prettiest thing about it, the headboard and pillows. I dislike seeing a bed in profile.

But in this room, I inherited a niche. The niche determined where the bed was going to be, which meant the first glimpse would be from the side. So to attract the eye to the pillows and headboard, I upholstered the niche in a nice linen damask. The tone-on-tone pattern is soft and pretty. It's an appealing combination with the creamy wainscoting, and it becomes this French country fantasy. You sense that you're in another time and place.

THE LITTLE-KNOWN FACT ABOUT BIG UPTOWN
apartments is that once you strip off the molding
and tear down some walls, you've got a loft. All
those stately buildings are really skeletal steel-frame
structures. So it's not surprising that as the loft
ethos caught on in New York, it moved uptown,
into the hearts, minds, and floor plans of Upper East
Side and West Side residents. I respect classical
architecture, but some of those once-grand prewar
apartments now look a little dowdy. They could
use the uplift you get from a more youthful point
of view.

When my client called about remodeling the
kitchen in his uptown apartment, he said he wanted
the sense of a casual loft that would feel both
sophisticated and relaxed. The kitchen had already
been renovated by previous owners, so there was
nothing original. We started fresh and gave it a new
focus with a breakfast counter made of a long, thin
slab of Absolute Black granite suspended between
two columns. This element anchors the far end of
the kitchen, on the way to the dining room. The wall
behind the counter can slide open or closed. With
the wall open to the dining room, the counter could
work as a serving table, or for simple grazing during
a buffet. It's a natural place for kids to hang out. A
large rectangular lampshade over the counter
completed the setting. The aesthetic was utilitarian,
like a loft, so in the spirit of not trying to hide
anything, we parked two stainless-steel storage units
below. Black-seated stools on stainless-steel supports
provide seating. I stained the floor black, creating,
with the elegantly thin granite and steel framework
of the breakfast bar, what turned out to be a
Mondrianesque composition of black and white.

I love cantilevered objects, whether they're decks
outside or counters inside. Your brain tells you
something is supporting it, but the eye tells you it's
floating in midair, magically.

I lined both sides of the kitchen proper with
teak cabinets. Thin lines of steel inserted into the
wood create just the suggestion of traditional panels.
The wall behind the stove is made of concrete,
and a huge steel backsplash rises from the stove to
the exhaust hood. Open stainless-steel shelves cross
the concrete wall and backsplash. A professional
stainless-steel refrigerator and stove continue the
industrial theme.

When I lay floors, I use the pattern either to
elongate or to widen a room, depending on whether
the space is too short or too narrow. The direction
of the flooring can reinforce the intention of the
design. In this case, I placed the planks to lead your
eye to the stove and up the wall.

ACKNOWLEDGMENTS

I WOULD LIKE TO ACKNOWLEDGE THE FOLLOWING FOR THEIR SUPPORT:

Christine Pittel, a friend and cowriter of this book. She makes it look so simple to turn words into poetry; Andrea Monfried and everyone at The Monacelli Press; Beverly Joel, who has helped see the flow in my projects and photographs; Benjamin Moore, for letting me use their colors to express my thoughts

THE MAGAZINES AND EDITORS-IN-CHIEF WHO HAVE ENCOURAGED AND PUBLISHED MY WORK:

Cindy Allen, *Interior Design*; Dara Caponigro, *Veranda*; Jason Kontos, *New York Spaces*; Margaret Russell, *Elle Décor*; Newell Turner, *House Beautiful*; Pilar Viladas, *The New York Times Magazine*

MY WONDERFUL CLIENTS AND FRIENDS—

especially the clients whose homes appear in the book—without whose endorsement and trust this would not be possible: Mr. Preston Bailey, Mr. and Mrs. Harvey Bernstein, Brack Capital Real Estate, Mr. and Mrs. Stanley Cook, Mr. Doug Davis, Mr. and Mrs. Fred Davis, Ms. Marie Douglas, Mr. and Mrs. Raymond Epstein, Mr. and Mrs. Frank Greenberg, Jyll and John, Mr. and Mrs. Norman Leben, Mr. and Mrs. Scott Markoff, Mr. and Mrs. Robert Meyrowitz, Mr. and Mrs. Richard Novick, Mr. and Mrs. Ronald Ostrow, Mr. and Mrs. Paul Pressler, Ms. Iva Spitzer, Mr. David Storper, Mr. and Mrs. Stephen Tobias, Mr. and Mrs. John Vickers, and Mr. and Mrs. Neil Weiss

AND THE TEAM AT VICENTE WOLF ASSOCIATES AND VW HOME:

Maureen Martin, Maureen McDermott, John Mistriotis, Susan Moolman, Jacqueline Pagan, Tina Ramchandani, David Rogal, and Trudi Romeo